RED SPIES IN WASHINGTON

RED SPIES IN WASHINGTON

George Carpozi, Jr.

TRIDENT PRESS · NEW YORK

To Chrysanthe, Julie, Elaine, Georgie, Harriette and Chrysie.

Contents

*Photographs appear following
pages 96 and 160.*

1

The Kremlin in Our Capital

On the Virginia shore of the broad Potomac aloof from the District of Columbia's vast acreage of governmental buildings, is that five-sided immensity—the Pentagon.

The sight of this colossus is something for tourists to talk about back home.

But if the Pentagon is the conversation piece of travelers, it is also the center of attention for another kind of Washington visitor, totally disinterested in its architectural merits. The lure is the vast storehouse of secret plans, military data, and security information within that enormous structure.

This "other" visitor is the spy of the Soviet Union, who comes to the nation's capital under a mantle of diplomatic immunity as an Embassy consul, diplomatic aide, clerk, typist, stenographer, translator, or other servant of statecraft. All are trained and equipped to function individually or collectively, depending on the mission for Moscow.

The Pentagon is not the only target of Soviet espionage, but it is the primary one, since it is the heart of America's military machine, with a staff of 30,000 military and civilian employees who constitute the commanding echelons of the Army, Navy, and Air Force.

Recurrent political truces and "détentes," periods of decreased tensions between the United States and the Union of Soviet Socialist Republics, in no way lessen the Kremlin's designs on our military, industrial, commercial, and cultural stores.

If anything, an era of good feeling tends to facilitate Soviet thrusts into our defense and security fabric, for the American— taking his cue from official channels in Washington which suddenly subscribe to the principle of good fellowship toward the Russians— is quick to relax his guard.

Yet the facts show that Soviet espionage is not influenced by changes in the political climate or the Cold War status. The Soviet Union appropriates an estimated two billion dollars in the annual budget for intelligence apparatus aimed at the United States alone —and the work must be carried out regardless of any *entente cordiale* that might exist from time to time between the two nations.

It is easy to see the justification of the warnings trumpeted repeatedly by J. Edgar Hoover, the vigilant director of the Federal Bureau of Investigation, who tells us that Soviet espionage in this decade has been more active and on a much broader scale than ever before.

It is a matter of necessity, indeed not inconceivably survival, for the Soviet Union to spy on us—just as we, for our own security and peace of mind, must and do spy on them. But the end results are not quite the same, principally because the Kremlin doesn't accord us the carte blanche freedom in their country that we extend to the Russians in ours. So we do not fall privy to as much intelligence— even with our widespread network of CIA agents.

In alerting the country to the escalating intensity of Soviet espionage in the United States and the Western Hemisphere, Hoover has made it clear that Moscow's trained agents are engaged in spy activity here under any number of guises. In the more than two-score cases of Red espionage the FBI has cracked in the past twenty years, Kremlin agents have masqueraded as Soviet nationals touring the United States; as members of cultural groups; as employees of Amtorg, the Russian trade agency whose chief line of commerce is American secrets; as diplomatic representatives and aides, and as independent agents in the traditional cloak-and-dagger manner.

In a previous book, *Red Spies in the U.N.,* the author together with the late Pierre J. Huss focused on Soviet and satellite nation espionage as it emanates from the United Nations. We presented nineteen official cases in which FBI investigation unearthed irrefutable evidence of subversion—and even a frightening conspiracy in sabotage (the Cuban-Soviet plot to blow up major installations, industrial complexes, and commercial establishments on the Eastern Seaboard).

In this book, the purpose is to focus America's and the world's attention on Soviet and satellite nation espionage as it exists and functions in Washington.

Just as the Soviet Mission to the U.N. is the nerve center of Communist spy activity in New York and neighboring states, so is the Soviet Embassy the headquarters for espionage in Washington and its environs. However, it would be a mistake to conclude that the Soviet diplomatic establishments in Washington and New York have each been parceled their own "territory" to spy, and that rigid boundaries define the area within which each functions.

Actually, there are no lines of demarcation. Soviet agents from New York and Washington have traveled the continent to carry out their schemes, crisscrossing each other's paths as frequently as their missions dictate. A Russian agent stationed at the U.N. may find himself on assignment in Chicago at the very moment one of his counterparts from the nation's capital has arrived on another mission—or perhaps the same job, working together to cast confusing trails in the event their tracks have been picked up by the FBI.

While the U.N. Mission in New York and the Embassy in Washington are the Kremlin's principal bases of subversive movement in this country, the nerve center of Communist espionage is in the Soviet Union, in Moscow's Defense Ministry. It functions there as a sealed-off monolithic entity under the modest label of "the Intelligence Administration."

To the average Soviet citizen, the letters GPU identify this mysterious section but fail to explain its operations or objectives. The Muscovite is much better acquainted with the other initialed body, the KGB—standing for "Committee for State Security," the dreaded Soviet secret police—which is the domestic espionage agency delegated the primary duty of spying on the local body politic. Agents of the GPU are generally employed in espionage activities abroad.

How many intelligence agents comprise the worldwide Soviet espionage network is difficult to tell. But former United States Senator William Benton of Connecticut, now publisher of the *Encyclopædia Britannica Yearbook* and an expert on Soviet affairs, told the author that Russian candidates for espionage are under training constantly. He estimated that 50,000 future spies can be found at any given moment receiving basic indoctrination—in grade school!

Before graduation, the young prospects are screened and the brightest and most intelligent are sent to the notorious Marx-Engels Institute at Gorki.

First they are introduced to Communist ideology and ripened for fanatic loyalty. In this preliminary course, which lasts four months, there is little hint of the rigorous studies yet to come in molding the tough, unprincipled Kremlin agent.

The next phase covers a wide range of rougher activity, such as judo and fighting to kill. But the emphasis is on the use of weapons —portable guns, poison pistols, explosives, wiretapping, short-wave radio operation, photography and secret microfilm processing, use of hidden listening devices, and the fine art of sabotage.

Women, too, are taught here, their training touching on other ground. The techniques of seducing a male are just one facet of the curriculum, but an important one. The trainee who learns well this ancient art will reap dividends when she must apply her skill on a prospect who may have information the Soviets seek. For once a man is caught in a compromising position, the Marx-Engels tutors tell their undergraduates, he becomes a candidate for blackmail. The distaff side also is instructed in mixing drinks, particularly with drugs that will plunge victims into an easy state of babble.

All candidates are thoroughly oriented in the nature and habits of different peoples; they are taught to speak, to think, to act as natives of countries targeted for Soviet espionage.

Graduates of the Gorki school are assigned missions on a variety of levels. Some are delegated places with traveling cultural groups. Others enter the diplomatic corps. Still others are provided with forged passports and dispatched to this country to form cells comprising a handful of trained operatives—as a matter of general practice no more than ten—who receive instructions from higherups either in New York or the capital, or directly from Moscow.

In his revealing book, *Masters of Deceit,* FBI Director Hoover described two categories of agents. He characterized the first, the "legal" spy, as the accredited diplomat who controls an espionage network from the UN Mission or the Embassy, the second he called the "master" or "illegal" spy who works for the most part independently of "legal" conspirators from a command post that could be as inconspicuous as an export firm or as incongruous as the small shop of an antique dealer.

The classic example of the "illegal" spy was Soviet Colonel Rudolph Ivanovich Abel, of the Soviet Military Intelligence. He was unmasked by the FBI in 1957 after long years of espionage activity behind the facade of a small photography business in Brooklyn and the highly effective pose of his assumed name, Emil R. Goldfus.

The function of "illegal" agents is to buttress the espionage activities of the "legal" spies and be prepared to take over the subversive machinery in event of war or other emergency that would precipitate a severing of diplomatic relations.

While the "illegal" spies like Colonel Abel have had remarkable successes in this country, the vast majority of spy situations involve "legal" agents—the Soviet diplomats and Embassy employees.

Although the Pentagon is the strongest magnet for Soviet subversion here, it does not stand alone. Many other agencies in the capital are targets of espionage—the Department of Commerce, Department of Agriculture, the Patent Office, the State Department, the Central Intelligence Agency, Army Intelligence, National Security Agency, even the Justice Department and the FBI itself.

Moreover, Soviet intelligence-gathering operations do not always violate the law. The Russians are aware—as are most Americans —that one of the fruits of a democratic society is the bountiful crop of information available to the public at all times.

Thus it came as no great surprise when a defector not long ago told a U.S. Senate Subcommittee investigating Soviet espionage in this country that the ease with which information is obtained in the United States has drastically reduced the hazardous and time-consuming efforts that would otherwise have to be employed.

Another witness estimated that the Soviet military attaché's office in Washington is able to obtain—through legal channels—as much as ninety-five percent of the information devoured by the Kremlin. In contrast, he explained, an intelligence agent in any other country spends ninety percent of his time in sniffing out this type of data.

"The variety of information collected by Soviet agents is amazing," says FBI Director Hoover. "It is not only highly secret technical and military data, but such things as road maps, population statistics, transit systems, and penicillin production. In addition, the Soviets are interested in matters involving foreign policy, data regarding the personal lives of key national leaders, and Government policy decisions. In other words, their intelligence attack is total; it involves every facet of our national life."

There are many ways in which Soviet intelligence gathers this data. It assigns officials to attend conventions of aeronautical, electronics, plastics, educational, and innumerable other industrial, business, and cultural groups. They correspond with many chambers of commerce around the country, visit still others, even in small towns, and obtain maps, photographs, and industrial statistics. They buy Government documents, literally by the thousands, from the Government Printing Office, the Patent Office, and the Department of Commerce. And they correspond with American business firms and subscribe to all types of scientific and technical journals, business magazines, as well as industrial house organs and employee magazines, but particularly to newspapers—especially those published near military bases and areas Soviet citizens are not lawfully allowed to travel.

Perhaps a classic example of the Soviets' appetite for data is the case of the two Russians at one of the Western Electric Company conventions in Los Angeles. The gentlemen from Moscow came early and started collecting every available pamphlet and paper at the gathering. When the bulk became unwieldy, they deposited the material at a check stand and went back for more. The load of literature finally amassed by them was estimated to weigh 250 pounds. And it was all legal.

But the primary objective of Soviet espionage, of course, is the top-secret military information lodged in the Pentagon. Actually— as far as the author was able to determine—the Kremlin agents themselves have never penetrated the vast building. But it is not necessary to gain physical entrance to the Pentagon; other channels to Pentagon secrets are all too apparent to resourceful Red agents.

With the many thousands of employees in the various Government departments, Washington is a mine of information for enterprising Soviet spies. Countless opportunities are open to gather information or to make contacts with some misguided or disgruntled employee who, for a price, will sell out his country.

Fortunately there have been only a handful of Americans who fell prey to the massive, systematic, and purposeful approach of the Communists. But the information given by those who have has helped supply missing links in the mosaic of knowledge on America's defense or military intentions, pieced together over months and even years at the Soviet Embassy.

Offers of money, favors, or any appeal or tactic that will advance the Kremlin's aims have been used. It is all part of the broad Communist conspiracy to attain world supremacy and domination. The espionage-gathering machinery being exposed in this book is the chief propellant in the drive toward that goal.

It is the Kremlin's foothold in the capital. . . .

2

"Mr. Bold"

Washington is a ten o'clock town. And in dead of winter, it closes up even earlier.

Collectors of historical coincidence may someday read significance into the fact that the city is named for our first President; that he was a contemporary of Benjamin Franklin who wrote in his *Poor Richard's Almanac* the adage, "Early to bed and early to rise . . ." and that the city of Washington still rises and retires by the rules written by a wise revolutionary nearly two centuries ago.

But it is unlikely that the man who shuffled along the cold, windswept street one February evening of 1956 had ever heard of Franklin or his *Poor Richard's Almanac*. He might better have been able to recall the precisely defined words of his nation's modern-day founder, a spade-bearded revolutionary of another time and a more violent philosophy—Lenin.

The foreigner walked the Washington sidewalk with some familiarity. His briefings had been thorough, and he had been in the city long enough to confirm its unfailing pattern of life: four thirty P.M. —lights out in Federal office buildings; five P.M.—cocktail hour with long conversations, much impressing of one's acquaintances and business associates, lots of "mingling" with the right people in the right places, at the right time—this is the way to get ahead in Washington; seven P.M.—time to go home; cars fill the streets as officials and semi-officials in the nation's capital head for their homes where it is "lights out" by ten or ten thirty P.M., eleven at the latest.

The foreigner knew precisely when his prey would be most receptive. After all, a few martinis and anything was possible.

So it was close to eight o'clock that evening of February 20 when he came to the home of John Kent, who was just finishing dinner.

Boldly, for this was his style, the visitor rapped on the door. The area was the northeast section of the capital, and that is as close as we are permitted to pinpoint this citizen's residence. In fact John Kent isn't his real name. Both are being withheld to protect his identity. But everything else about this story is true.

A former Army officer, now a civilian employed as a Government engineer, John Kent could not ignore the compelling rat-a-tat-tat on the wooden door. He opened it to be confronted by a man he'd never seen.

"Are you Mr. Kent?" the stranger asked, his voice heavily accented. It has a Slavic sound, thought the ex-officer.

"Yes," said Kent. Then, politely, "Was there something you wanted?"

"I want talk to you something about military engineering. You are familiar, this subject, are you not?" the stranger replied in broken but understandable English.

Surprised by this straightforward approach, Kent was too much of a gentleman to slam the door in the man's face. Besides, he was curious. Who was this stranger bundled up against the cold, looking much like a Cossack with his fur hat pulled down almost to his ears, the collar of his great black coat shoved up high around his neck to keep the buffeting winds from his body?

"Won't you come in?" Kent offered.

"Thank you. Wery cold outside. Nice, varm here," the visitor said, removing his coat, placing his gray Persian hat alongside it on a chair, and walking into the living room which reflected the middle-class warmth and hospitality of the typical American home.

Kent looked at his visitor and mentally took note. This man is in his early thirties, he thought. Thirty-two to thirty-five years old— five feet six or seven. About 165 pounds, probably a little overweight judging by that slight bulge. Call him medium in build.

Kent also noted the man's brown hair and crystal-clear gray eyes, the fair complexion. Might be a Pole, or else a Czech.

He was right on almost every count, except the country the man came from.

"I am from Soviet Embassy," the visitor stated with the casual air of a salesman saying to a prospective client: "I'm from the Metropolitan Life Insurance Company."

Kent eyed him with some bewilderment. He couldn't fathom what someone from the Soviet Embassy would want with him.

"Well, sir, what's your name?"

"Krylov . . . here, I spell it." Taking a small slip of paper from his trouser pocket and a pen from the inside of his jacket, he carefully wrote, articulating as a schoolchild would, "K-r-y-l-o-v. See, Krylov."

The name meant nothing to Kent. He'd never heard of it. He knew no one from the Soviet Embassy.

"Why have you come to see me?" Kent asked. "Who sent you?"

"Man, his name Kyle. He said to come to see you."

"See me about what?" Kent interrupted with some annoyance. He had had a few moments to think, and it suddenly occurred to him that he had read this plot somewhere before. On frequent occasions he'd seen the *Washington Post* and the *Times-Herald* headlines about Soviet espionage.

"What are you after?" Kent was beginning to feel sorry he'd let the stranger into his house.

"Want to secure information about fortifications. Mr. Kyle say you are expert on fortifications," the Russian said easily.

Kent couldn't believe his ears. From all that he'd read and heard about Soviet espionage, he'd never once come across such a brazen approach for military information. Kent decided to humor the man. This might, after all, be a prank by one of his friends.

"Just what kind of fortifications are you interested in?"

"Want to know about military fortifications. I have made efforts in many places to gather information. Even go to Library of Congress . . . but man there told me he have nothing to help me. That is why I come to you, Mr. Kent. I think maybe you have old books, or maybe magazines. You know what I mean?"

If this was a joke, Kent realized, it had gone far enough. But he had the distinct feeling this man was genuine. And he was right. Krylov was very much genuine. Had he wanted, he could have identified himself more fully as Yuri P. Krylov, captain in the army of the Union of Soviet Socialist Republics. He had arrived in Washington nine months earlier, on May 4, 1955, and been assigned to the office of the Soviet military attaché.

For more than an hour, under the friendliest of attitudes, Krylov conducted a wide-ranging conversation which covered many areas. He spoke in that difficult-to-understand broken English, which was about the only thing about Krylov that was phony, for in fact he could speak almost flawless English.

Krylov placed heaviest emphasis on his desire to obtain information about military fortifications, but there were many other favors he wanted.

He was very anxious to join the Society for American Military Engineers. Could Kent help?

Agriculture was a continuing headache for his native land. Was Kent familiar with the Russian plan for improving wheat production? Had he heard about Premier Khrushchev's ambitious program to convert the virgin lands to real agricultural production? Did Kent have any ideas where Krylov could put his hands on American agricultural production methods?

Krylov talked on, not always asking for something. He steered himself into a discussion about cultural exchange visits between America and Russia. Didn't Kent agree that these helped foster better relations between the people of the two countries?

And had he ever wanted to visit the Soviet Union? "If you went, you would see how we are trying to do the best for our people," the Russian said proudly.

There was a shrewd method to this seeming rambling, sometimes disconnected thread of conversation. Krylov was feeling his way along the uncertain corridor to subversion.

If he could strike a responsive chord in the man with whom he spoke, a receptive interest in anything they discussed, this would become the "bond" which could tie the two men together for the future.

If Krylov were able to do nothing more with Kent's help than sign up for a membership in a technical society, that in itself would be an achievement.

But this night at John Kent's home was a wasted visit for Krylov. Wary of his propositioner, understandably puzzled and apprehensive, Kent wasn't buying anything Krylov offered.

With a too-hearty "Good-bye, good-bye," Krylov walked out into the cold darkness and out of Kent's life—and right into the FBI's. For the instant the Russian left, Kent was on the phone to the FBI's Washington bureau to tell about the incredible Soviet visitor. Agents came to Kent's house and obtained a full report.

And when they checked and found that there was, in fact, a Yuri P. Krylov in the office of the Soviet military attaché, that his description fitted the man who had come to see John Kent, agents were quickly put on the Russian's tail.

The G-men soon found to their surprise that Krylov was bent on entering the lives of other Americans. They shadowed him to other Washington homes where approaches almost carbon-copied after his visit to Kent were repeated. His advances were almost foolish bravado. The phones at the FBI offices kept ringing with calls from Washingtonians, like John Kent.

It wasn't long before Krylov was a full-blown case in FBI files. And by then the G-men had their favorite nickname for him. They were calling him "Mr. Bold." And he was indeed the boldest spy the FBI had ever encountered.

Krylov must have felt he had a good thing going for him because he never deviated from the technique he had used on John Kent. At times he was even bold enough to venture directly into the offices of those he saw as potential sources of information.

When he wanted data on the field of atomic energy, he thought nothing of walking into the office of a member of the Atomic Energy Commission, offering to hire him as a consultant to the Russians!

This approach was as subtle as a lead pipe in the hands of a mugger. And people were usually stunned by the quick, heavy-handed swing as Krylov went right to the heart of the matter in his quest for information.

Krylov plunged onward in his efforts to make "contacts" in Washington, but then he tried to go further. Two months after he first came to the FBI's attention, Krylov introduced himself in his familiar way to the manager of a Washington electronics supply house, seeking more than information—he wanted to buy hard-to-get electronic equipment.

It was mid-afternoon of April 19 that Krylov entered on this new tack, with a style that almost floored the manager.

"My name Krylov," he smiled benevolently. "I want to buy

some electronic tubes. I have list in my pocket."

The Russian handed a sheet of paper to the manager. It listed radio and television tubes, transistors, condensers, and other material that could be used in both military and non-military equipment.

It wasn't the list of items that shocked the manager, but the paper on which it was written—the stationery of the Soviet Embassy.

"Are you with the Embassy?" the manager asked.

"Yes," Krylov replied in a low voice, looking around to see if he was being overheard. "I know what you are going to ask me, but I want to speak to you alone. Can we go someplace?"

The manager wanted to find out if the tubes and other materials were to be shipped to the Soviet Union. Undoubtedly they were, because large quantities were designated.

And the next question the manager had to ask, because it was the law, was whether Krylov or the Russians had secured a license to legally export this electronic equipment to the Soviet Union.

Of course, the material was going to Russia; but, regrettably, the Soviets didn't have the license. The bulk of the items Krylov was trying to obtain were embargoed for shipment to the Soviet Union. Thus, again, Krylov's actions had the distinct ring of subversion.

The manager felt impelled to turn him away with a flat refusal to do business. But he had the presence of mind to tell himself this wasn't the way to handle the situation.

If I refuse him these parts, the manager reasoned, he'll go somewhere else. He'll keep trying until he finds someone unscrupulous enough to work the deal Krylov suggested.

The deal that Krylov wanted was simple in its refinement—it offered a fat "commission" for every sale the manager made to him, an under-the-counter payment that no one but Krylov and the manager would know about.

In the privacy of his office where he had invited the Russian to "talk this over," the manager agreed to work with Krylov. But there would be a "slight hitch," as the manager put it, which might delay delivery of the order a few weeks.

"You see," he said, "some of these items are out of stock and we don't expect them in until the second week in May."

"Oh, that is all right," Krylov countered. "I am not in hurry. I wait."

The manager had set the trap. In his mind he'd already plotted what he was going to do. He rose to his feet and shook hands warmly with Krylov as he showed him to the door. When the Russian was gone, the manager went back to his desk and phoned the FBI.

Agents who had been on Krylov's trail had actually followed him to the electronic supply firm's headquarters. But they couldn't know what had gone on inside. They merely noted the stop in their growing dossier on Krylov and when he came out took after him to his next destination. Later, back at the FBI offices, they would turn in their report and a superior routinely would send other agents to the electronics place to inquire what Krylov was doing there.

In this case, however, there was no need to send investigators. The FBI had already been informed by the manager. He was promptly enlisted to serve as a double agent for the Bureau. Arrangements were made to let Krylov believe he was getting away with his scheme so more could be learned about his operations. By letting him get away with illicit purchases at the Washington electronics supply house, the FBI hoped to unearth evidence of similar transactions—if such existed—with other distributors that investigators were not aware of.

The manager had the order all but entirely filled by May 10 when the Russian dropped by the office to check on delivery. Everything on the list had first been cleared by the FBI. The few remaining items that the manager said had not come in yet were purposely held back because the Government didn't want them in Russian hands.

"We are having difficulty filling orders on these items," the manager apologized. "But I'm doing my best and as soon as they come in I'll deliver them to you."

Krylov seemed extremely pleased with his initial success, incomplete as it was.

"Will you phone me at the Embassy when the balance of the order arrives?" Krylov asked, his English now almost flawless.

The manager said he would. Then Krylov picked up the sales slip which was made out in triplicate. He glanced at the blank provided for the purchaser's name. It was made out to "Cash." Krylov liked that.

"I see you have found a way to deliver this material to me without getting yourself in trouble," he said.

The manager had been advised to handle the sale that way to show the Soviet spy he was trying to avoid involvement in an illicit transaction. That would make an impression on Krylov and perhaps lull him into believing the manager was willing to do anything for the Russian, if the price was right.

"This puts me on the spot," the manager said with consternation. "I can get into a great deal of trouble if they find out what I'm doing."

He'd been told to say this. Obviously it was a pitch for a bribe. For once the Russians pay their corrupt money to an American, they feel he is in their "pocket" and will not likely blow the whistle. They also sustain the belief then that the corrupted American is trapped deeply enough to yield to their demands for bigger favors, and if he doesn't he can be threatened with blackmail.

The manager didn't have to draw pictures for Krylov who leaped to his feet and dug his hand into the inside pocket of his jacket. He pulled out an envelope and withdrew a quantity of twenty-dollar bills, all crisply new from the bank. Krylov looked at the amount on the sales slip, $286.50.

"Here," he said, counting out the twenties. "This will take care of the company—and this will make you happy."

He counted out fifteen of the twenties into one pile, amounting to three hundred dollars, then placed a single twenty beside them.

"With the thirteen dollars and fifty cents change from this," Krylov said, pointing to the larger pile of cash, "you will put it here and together that will give you a handsome commission." Krylov indicated with his finger the lone twenty-dollar bill. With the balance of the three hundred dollars added to it, the manager was left $33.50 as a "commission," or roughly twelve percent of the sale price—extremely high as sales bonuses go in legitimate enterprise.

"I'm very grateful to you, Mr. Krylov," the manager said. "This makes it worth the risk I'm taking. I hope we can continue this excellent business relationship."

The stage was set for the next exchange which came October 4, after Krylov had phoned the manager at his office and asked to meet him that evening in nearby West Hyattsville, Maryland.

"I have good reason not to come to your place," Krylov said cryptically. "I think it is better if we talk about my next order someplace where we can be alone."

The manager was uncertain whether to accept the invitation. He had been advised to notify the FBI in case anything unusual came up.

"Listen, Mr. Krylov," the manager said, "I've got to check with my wife. She had invited some folks over for tonight and I want to make certain she'll tolerate my absence. Is there somewhere I can call you back?"

Krylov said he'd phone again in fifteen minutes.

That gave the manager enough time to dial the FBI agent handling the case. The advice was "meet him."

The rendezvous was scheduled by Krylov for seven P.M. at the corner of Queens Chapel Road and Hamilton Street in West Hyattsville. Both men drove there in their own cars, parked nearby, and walked to their destination.

Krylov greeted the manager with a hearty handshake and a remarkably fluent flow of conversation, a sharp contrast to the almost illiterate style of speaking he had employed on his first contact with the American that April day back at the electronics supply house. In fact, the Russian never again resorted to that feigned dialect in his dealings with the manager. Krylov apparently felt he could make greater gains by being himself.

"I have picked out a nice restaurant for dinner," Krylov told the somewhat surprised manager. Then magnanimously with a sweep of his hand, Krylov added, "And it will all be on me. I've been asked by my superior to compliment you on the excellent efforts you have made, and he wants me to show you his gratitude."

Krylov took the manager by the arm and escorted him to a restaurant down the street. They ordered cocktails, dinner, and cordials in a meal that lasted until ten fifteen P.M. During that time Krylov did most of the talking almost entirely on business. Krylov had an important order that he wanted filled. It was itemized on a long yellow sheet he took from his pocket and put on the table in front of the manager. "This is quite an order," the manager said to Krylov, shaking his head. "It's going to take quite a while to fill it. I'm not even certain I can get some of these parts—"

Krylov put up his hand in a gesture to interrupt the manager.

"Please, do not worry about rushing. I will be glad to receive delivery in a month. There is no hurry."

Krylov was told it would take at least that long and perhaps longer.

"You have some items here that may involve Government clearance," the manager said. "They would involve an explanation about where the material is going . . . and in your case I certainly can't do that."

Krylov said he understood and asked the manager to do the best he could.

It wasn't until November 13 that Krylov's order was prepared for delivery. The manager phoned the Embassy.

"I will not come to your office," Krylov said. "Do as I tell you. Take the order to your house this evening, leave it there, then drive to the forty-three-hundred block of Rhode Island Avenue in Brentwood [just outside Washington in Maryland]. I will be waiting for you."

The manager didn't have to check with the FBI this time. He had been told to meet Krylov whenever he called for a personal confrontation away from the electronics firm—but to notify the FBI of any such arrangement so agents could be assigned on a surveillance.

Krylov's request was unusual in wanting the material brought to the manager's house. But it didn't faze the FBI. Krylov was merely employing an old Soviet espionage tactic, a measure of safety against detection. The Bureau knew that Krylov would meet the manager, take him to dinner, then in all likelihood they would leave together for his home to pick up the material. Meanwhile, another Red agent would observe the initial meeting on the street and attempt to observe whether Krylov and the manager were being followed—by the FBI.

In changing the routine for delivery, Krylov inadvertently diminished what slender chance the Soviets had of spotting his FBI tail. The G-men simply took even greater precautions than they normally do to avoid detection. They fell back far enough so as to spot the Russian who had been sent out to spot them!

Krylov was his usual cordial, affable self at dinner in a restaurant in Brentwood. He complimented the manager profusely for delivering the hard-to-get electronics parts and promised "greater rewards in the future." In fact, the twenty-eight dollars "commission" on the three-hundred-fifty-dollar order was scarcely worth the trouble the manager had gone to.

But then, historically, the Soviets have always been atrociously frugal payers. One of the great mysteries surrounding the whole field of espionage has been how the Kremlin gets anyone to betray his country for the kind of depressed wages they pay.

But the manager was not out to make money in his dealings with Krylov. And there was no point in demanding more because the FBI had decided that Krylov had gone as far as he should be allowed. This was to be the last order the Russian would place.

There was enough evidence against Krylov, the FBI had decided, to put the case up to the State Department. When Krylov accompanied the manager to his house in Laurel, Maryland, after dinner in Brentwood, hidden FBI cameras with infrared film recorded the delivery to the Russian.

That documentation, coupled with the other evidence gathered over the months the FBI had been following Krylov on his busy rounds in Washington and its suburbs, was more than enough to bring action.

The State Department delivered a note to the Soviet Embassy on January 14, 1957, which declared Yuri P. Krylov persona non grata for his illicit activities in his capacity as a diplomatic envoy. Three days later, with bag packed, Krylov started for home to rejoin his wife, Galina, and son, Pavel, in Leningrad.

It was another cold winter's day in Washington when Krylov departed—but it was much colder in Leningrad. Even the warmth of his family's welcome probably could not take away the chill reception awaiting him at the Kremlin for his failure as a spy.

But back in Washington things were much quieter again. Without Krylov around knocking on doors in the middle of the night, without the FBI phones ringing with calls from citizens to complain about the strange spy from Russia who dropped in on them uninvited, the city once again was back to its old self as a ten o'clock town.

3

The Hands-Across-the-Sea Spy Case

The Washington Monument stands as an unadorned shaft of pure marble reaching over 500 feet into the sky. During daylight hours it is a mecca for tourists who ride the elevator to the top for a view of our capital and vast stretches of its surrounding country-side. After dark, however, the brilliantly lighted obelisk, although visible for miles, is usually deserted.

Shortly after seven o'clock on the evening of Tuesday, April 12, 1951, a solitary figure emerged from the darkness and headed up the grassy incline to the base of the monument. On his left hand he wore a brown leather glove; on his right, a band of adhesive tape around the middle finger like a ring. Tucked under his left arm was a red-jacketed book.

This was Herbert Norrison, a twenty-nine-year-old American with a wife and family and a job in Washington. The only thing that would set him apart from any other average citizen in the nation's capital was that he had a sensitive position with a Government agency.

And he was involved in a strange case of espionage—the first to lead directly to the Soviet Embassy in Washington and the first involving an attempt to steal military secrets.

Moments after his arrival, another figure appeared out of the darkness some fifty feet away.

As soon as Norrison spotted the newcomer, he raised his gloved left hand to adjust the book under his arm and lifted his right hand to scratch his ear so the taped middle finger could be distinguished readily. The two men had never met before and Norrison's glove, adhesive tape, and book were simply the trappings of recognition.

The second figure, a lighted cigarette dangling from the right side of his thickish lips, approached with slow, unhesitating steps, until he brought himself face to face with Norrison.

"Hello, is the Monument closed tonight?" he asked in accordance with the prearranged code of recognition.

Herbert Norrison replied with equal care, "It will reopen tomorrow morning."

They had made their contact as planned and the next move was to walk together back into the shadows to accomplish the main purpose of the meeting—the transmission of Government data relating to the U.S. Air Force. Herbert Norrison had brought a small, unmarked, white business-size envelope containing eight single-spaced typewritten sheets of paper which listed names of Air Force officers and enlisted personnel destined for transfer to the American Overseas Forces in Austria.

The man to whom Norrison handed the packet wasn't known to him. He had never seen him before. But he knew that he was an agent for the Soviet Union and all his dealings in the future would be with him, or others designated by him. Norrison was told by his contact almost immediately to call him Yuri. No last name was mentioned.

Actually this was Yuri V. Novikov, Second Secretary at the Soviet Embassy in Washington and the main cog in a daring plot to obtain information pertaining not only to the transfers of Air Force personnel but also covering the gamut of U.S. military and intelligence activities in Washington as well as Austria. In fact, the meeting between Norrison and Novikov had been arranged in Vienna by two American citizens who had worked out every last detail down to the time and place and even the wording of the coded greeting.

Otto Verber and Kurt L. Ponger were native-born Viennese who had emigrated to the United States during the late 1930s and settled in New York City. After becoming naturalized citizens, they had served in the U.S. Army during World War II, then had returned to Vienna, supposedly for schooling under the GI Bill.

Their recruitment into the ranks of Soviet espionage bears an unusual and ironic twist. Here were two immigrants who had found sanctuary in the United States from the persecution and tyranny of Nazi dictatorship. Yet in 1949, they inexplicably sold out to the Reds and became traitors against their adopted country. In historical retrospect, the yoke of Naziism was hardly less subjugative or oppressive in its time than the rule of Josef Stalin in the year of 1949.

Perhaps it is well to look at each man's background so as to lend some human significance to the impersonal language in the diary of betrayal Otto Verber and Kurt L. Ponger wrote for themselves.

Ponger was born July 29, 1913, the son of a moderately prosperous jeweler and goldsmith. He was educated in Viennese public elementary and secondary schools, participated in athletics, and was active in the Austrian Boy Scout movement which, according to Central Intelligence Agency information, he "propagandized with his radical views." This allegation of fanaticism is not explained further in the dossier on his early background. Nor is much more known about his youth. The only other child in the family was a girl, Margaretta.

In his late teens, Ponger served an apprenticeship in the jeweler's and goldsmith's trades, following in his father's footsteps. In the early 1930s, Kurt Ponger became active in the ranks of the Austrian Social-Democratic Party. At about that time, too, he began courting Vera Verber, Otto's attractive elder sister.

The romance was fated to succeed, for the Ponger and Verber families were friends, and the parents on both sides campaigned for the marriage of their children.

The close family ties also brought Kurt into association with Otto, eight years his junior. Kurt, who had retained his strong early interest in athletics, took Otto in hand and trained him in gymnastics and other sports, then led him into the Boy Scouts.

Like Kurt, young Otto also attended Vienna's public schools. His father, a well-to-do attorney in the Austrian capital, had no special political leanings. He was possessed only by the desire to practice law and to see justice dispensed to his clients.

The absorbing attention Ponger lavished on Verber in those early days became a sort of big-brother relationship and served as the springboard for Kurt's influence and, indeed, domination of Otto in later years.

The late 1930s brought on increasingly difficult times for the Ponger and Verber families, as they did for most Austrians. The menace of Nazi Germany, and the constant fear of what would happen to persons of the Jewish faith, like the Pongers and Verbers, reduced their daily lives to a constant nightmare of fear.

Their anxieties became dread realities in March, 1938, when Germany annexed Austria.

The Verbers escaped to England, then emigrated to the United States, settling in New York City. But daughter Vera, who also fled with her parents, chose to stay in London.

The Pongers were not as fortunate. They took their chances in Vienna and came under the heel of Nazi persecution. While his parents and sister escaped arrest, Kurt did not. He was seized by Austrian police acting under German orders in April, 1938, presumably because of his reputation as a radical. With 2,000 others, he was herded aboard a train guarded by German S.S. troops and shipped to the infamous Dachau concentration camp near Munich.

In mid-September, 1938, he was transferred to another notorious camp, Buchenwald, where he remained until March, 1939. Then he was released—on his promise not to remain in Germany or Austria and to keep silent about details of his imprisonment. Ponger, however, obtained a British visa through an international organization assisting refugees and returned to Vienna for an eight-day visit with his parents. Afterward he proceeded via Germany and Holland to England, and was reunited with Vera in London.

While there, he joined in the activities of the Austrian Center. He worked with the left-wing Austrian Youth Group, built up an association with various known Communists and other radical elements, then became a member of a Communist Party cell.

Vera Verber departed for New York City in January, 1940, and Ponger followed her from London a month later. Shortly afterward they were married and settled down in a comfortable four-room apartment at 773 Columbus Avenue in Manhattan.

Otto Verber, who had arrived in New York almost two years previously, married a fellow Austrian refugee, Eva Beer in 1942 and settled down. They had gone to live in a fifty-dollar-a-month three-room flat in a five-story brownstone at 8 West 105th Street, not far from where the Pongers took up residence.

Like their parents, the new generation Pongers and Verbers maintained a close relationship which led them to take an interest in Austrian refugees in the New World. After some months they organized the Austro-American Youth Club to "unify" young exiles from their homeland.

Actually, according to the FBI which had an eye on this movement at the time, once Ponger and Verber had established the club, they proceeded to develop within its structure three distinct Communist cells. But their progress ended with America's entry into

World War II. Ponger and Verber were called up for military service—which, incidentally, would entitle them to naturalization.

Verber was summoned first. He was inducted in February, 1943, and because of an exceptionally high IQ rating was selected for officer training school. He went through the course with excellent grades, was commissioned a second lieutenant, then assigned to U.S. Army Intelligence. By the beginning of 1944 he was in Europe, taking part in General Eisenhower's sweep toward Berlin. En route Verber won the Bronze Star and, when the war was over, asked for separation. In December, 1945, he was honorably discharged and returned to his wife in New York.

Ponger was drafted in June, 1943, and was sent to the European theater, too, where he served as a corporal and an interrogator of German prisoners of war. He returned to civilian life in March, 1945, and came back to the United States.

Instead of taking up his old line as a costume jeweler, at which he had worked before going into the Army, Ponger entered a totally alien field—selling American newspapers, books, periodicals, and pamphlets to Central Europe. This operation is clouded by a lack of information. However, it is known that a corporation was formed by Ponger, under the impressive title of "Central European Press & Literary Agency Inc." There was no office, only a mailing address established on October 23, 1946, with the Huntley Business Service, at 100 West 42nd Street, Manhattan. Although Ponger had filed the application for Huntley's address service, he listed his wife, Vera, as president of the Central European Agency.

Among his known "employees" was another Austrian-born ex-GI, who at the time was twenty-five years old and attending one of the local city colleges.

Whether the agency sent radical or Communist-tainted propaganda to the Central European regions it claimed to service is not known. But Ponger evidently hadn't abandoned his leftist ventures. A tenant in the building where Ponger lived told the author: "He was constantly going around sticking Communist pamphlets and literature under the doors of apartments in the neighborhood."

What Verber did on his return from the Army is even less clear. There is indication he may have joined his brother-in-law in the Central European Press Agency, for at a later time he represented himself as a photographer of the firm.

Suddenly in November, 1946, Ponger, Verber and their families packed their belongings and left for Germany.

While the Pongers vacated their apartment and surrendered the lease, the Verbers subleased their quarters to a young man named Walter Lauber, of whom this is not the last mention.

Inexplicably, Ponger and Verber both had obtained civilian employment with the International War Crimes Tribunal in Nuremberg. Ponger got a job in the office of the chief counsel and Verber became an interrogator with the tribunal.

Then in the early fall of 1948, with the tribunal's work done, Verber and Ponger moved their families to Vienna and took up residence in an American sector of the city. Both men enrolled under the GI Bill as students at the University of Vienna, with Verber taking full-time courses; Ponger, part-time. But both men were granted Veterans Administration benefits covering tuition and subsistence allowance for the support of themselves and their families while going to college.

Ponger didn't take a full course because he had the settled purpose of continuing with his Central European Press Agency. He opened an office-studio in the Soviet zone of Vienna, and proceeded to free-lance for Austrian Socialist and Communist functions. He also collaborated with his wife in the publication of a literary-photographic journal.

Brother-in-law Otto Verber also devoted some spare time to the venture, for it was about this time that he represented himself as a photographer of the agency. Curiously, Central had continued to maintain its mailing address at Huntley Business Service in New

York, although there had been very few phone calls, messages, or letters for the agency after the move to Europe. Huntley was asked finally to discontinue the service in 1949. But on May 8, 1952, Central was suddenly revived by a new applicant, listed in Huntley's records as George Mandler, of New Haven, Connecticut.

It was in February, 1949, that Ponger apparently was recruited into the ranks of Soviet intelligence as an active agent, although there is some suspicion he may have worked for them in a minor capacity prior to that date.

The enlistment was effected officially, at least, by a Russian named Vladimir Greshnev, who was posing as a Czechoslovakian foreign correspondent. A month later, through Ponger's efforts and influence, Verber also agreed to become a spy for the Kremlin.

In essence, Verber was much better recruit material than Ponger because for some reason Otto had a great many more contacts than Kurt among the U.S. Forces in Austria and the American college students in Vienna.

Working at first under Ponger's guiding hand, Verber recruited his initial and most valuable source of intelligence information in Vienna—Herbert Norrison.

Norrison was with the Military Intelligence Service in Vienna and had access to considerable intelligence data. What made him an easy mark for Verber was that they had served together on the military tribunal at Nuremberg and were good friends.

Verber propositioned Norrison to supply intelligence information—for a price. Norrison agreed.

Following Soviet orders, Verber first requested a list of informants working with the Military Intelligence Service. About two weeks later, on June 18, 1949, Norrison delivered such a list.

Norrison was immediately given his next assignment—to supply the names of employees with the U.S. Forces in Austria, known better by its initials, USFA. The data were delivered a month later, on July 19.

The next request was for information about an American intelligence operative who was providing MIS with information about Red military activity in the Soviet sector of the city. When Verber received a document about this individual on August 3, he promptly asked Norrison to come up with a logistics and military capability fact sheet on USFA. On September 26, the information was handed to Verber who paid a thousand dollars for Norrison's services thus far.

But more information was sought—data about the national defense capability of the United States, top-secret intelligence reports on various phases of U.S. military activity and troop movements in Austria and Europe, U.S. intelligence files dealing with Russian installations and Russian military capabilities, and even a dossier on the whereabouts and activity of a defected Soviet airman in the United States. And more cash was handed to Herbert Norrison by Verber.

So far Verber had done all the work. And Ponger's role was to remain passive for the first year and a half.

But a day came in December, 1950, which was to activate Ponger.

"They're sending me back to the States," Norrison informed Verber at what had appeared a routine meeting. "I guess I'm out of business with you from here on in. I'll be leaving in a week."

Verber was stunned. But without even consulting his superiors, Verber quickly proposed to Norrison that he did not have to give up his role in espionage.

"Where are they sending you?" Verber asked.

"To Washington."

"Why, that's great," Verber was enthusiastic. "You'll be able to carry on . . . on even a larger scale. Undoubtedly you're going to be stationed in the Pentagon. Isn't that so?"

Norrison nodded. "I imagine that's where I'll be."

"Great!" Verber went on. "Now all I've got to do is get you a new set of instructions—and a contact in Washington."

This meeting took place in the early evening of December 29. The two men parted with the understanding that in a day or so Verber would have orders for Norrison on how to operate in the nation's capital.

Verber got in touch with his superior—Vladimir Greshnev, the Russian posing as a Czechoslovakian correspondent—and found that Norrison's new assignment posed a problem that was too big to be handled at that level.

"I will have to consult others and let you know what is to be done," the Russian told Verber.

The next day, December 30, Norrison was called by Verber. He was to meet Ponger and accompany him to Salzburg, about 170 miles east of Vienna. On New Year's Day, 1951, they went by train and there, in a small chalet-type home, found themselves at a meeting with Verber's Russian contact and two other persons—but not Verber.

One of the two has been identified by authorities as Mrs. Theresa Harris, the thirty-year-old stepdaughter of a Viennese city councillor and former newspaper editor named Rudolph Holzer, and a girlhood friend of Eva Beer, now Verber's wife. In 1938, at the age of sixteen, Theresa Holzer had fled Hitlerism and gone to London where she married an Englishman and had a son. But the marriage failed and she went back with her boy to Vienna where she got a job as a civilian secretary for the U.S. Army's military police battalion.

The other newcomer at the meeting was a slight, small-boned young man with hair that was thick and solidly brown and a sharply handsome, almost pretty face. His name was Walter Lauber—the same Walter Lauber who had taken the lease on the Verbers' apartment in New York when they had gone to Nuremberg.

What was he doing in Austria?—attending college in Vienna on the GI Bill, as Verber and Ponger had been doing. And also involved in espionage!

The meeting was held in an atmopshere of high intrigue as

Greshnev, Lauber, and Ponger hammered out the details of Herbert Norrison's Stateside tour as an agent of the Kremlin. Two problems required immediate resolution. One was to establish a contact for Norrison in Washington; the second was to find a suitable replacement for Norrison in the Military Information Service in Vienna.

"Is there anyone you can trust and recommend to us?" Vladimir asked.

Norrison said he hadn't considered anyone to fill his shoes, but if need be he'd try to find a candidate.

"Do that and bring his name to us the next time we meet."

The group then took up the question of assignment for Norrison when he got to Washington. But that was to depend upon his new post. Unquestionably he'd continue in MIS, but he couldn't know what his precise duties would be until he got there. Yet the matter of a contact had to be settled before Norrison left.

"We still have to look into that and give you instructions before you leave," Greshnev told him.

They agreed to meet again in Salzburg three days later, on January 4. This time Verber was present, but Ponger wasn't there. He was to arrive later.

"Did you find anyone to take your place in Vienna?" asked Vladimir.

"No one I can really trust," Norrison replied. "But I have a list of three names. Perhaps you may be able to cultivate one of them. I think they are all good prospects."

He reached into his inside jacket pocket, pulled out a small scrap of paper on which were scribbled the names of three Americans stationed with MIS in Vienna, and handed it to Greshnev.

The Russian glanced at the names. "Can we approach them?"

Norrison nodded. "I think you can."

"Well, if not, Otto might find a good man," Vladimir smiled. "After all, he discovered you. And you are the best."

The Russian, who was sitting on the sofa beside Norrison, drew out a thick wad of American money from his wallet and offered it to Norrison.

"This is for you, my friend," Vladimir said, watching carefully for the American's reaction.

Norrison reached out eagerly. He took the bills and flipped the edge of them with his thumb in the manner of a bank teller examining a bundle of new money. Norrison saw only twenty-dollar bills, and it appeared that there were at least a hundred.

"Two thousand?" he leaned forward keenly.

Vladimir snickered. "You should work in the Treasury Department. A perfect count!"

The doorbell rang at this point and Vladimir got up to answer. It was Ponger. He walked in, very businesslike, greeted the guests with a curt hello, and sat beside Norrison.

"These are your orders. Read them carefully. Memorize them. Then tear them up." Ponger handed Norrison a small white sheet of paper. On it was written in block letters:

SEVEN O'CLOCK AT NIGHT, TUESDAY, APRIL 12, MEET YOUR CONTACT AT WASHINGTON MONUMENT. WEAR BROWN LEATHER GLOVE ON LEFT HAND. KEEP OTHER GLOVE IN YOUR POCKET. HAVE RIGHT MIDDLE FINGER COVERED WITH PIECE OF ADHESIVE TAPE LIKE A RING. CARRY BOOK WITH RED COVER UNDER LEFT ARM. WAIT AT MONUMENT. CONTACT WILL APPROACH YOU. HE WILL SAY, "HELLO, IS THE MONUMENT CLOSED TONIGHT?" YOU WILL REPLY: "IT WILL REOPEN TOMORROW MORNING." HE WILL THEN TELL YOU HIS NAME IS YURI. DESTROY THESE ORDERS WHEN YOU HAVE MEMORIZED THEM.

Herbert Norrison sat back, reading the instructions closely. He looked at Ponger after a few moments and said, "I will have to hold onto this paper a while. I want to study the orders carefully."

"Just as long as it does not fall into the wrong hands," Ponger said, and then smiled. "But you are too good to let that happen."

Ponger rose to his feet. "Gentlemen," he said, "if there is nothing else to discuss we should adjourn. Herbert must get ready for his departure."

Norrison was leaving Austria for the States the next morning on an Air Force flight. He did not know this yet—but Verber did, and he had told Ponger. Verber's pipeline into the base provided him with plane schedules and flight manifests from the military side which even Norrison couldn't get.

Verber, Ponger, and Lauber rode on the train with Norrison back to Vienna. On the way, Ponger had further orders for the American—orders that could not be put in writing.

"You are going to be stationed in the Pentagon," Verber said, with the certainty that comes of knowing the inside of MIS activity. "Therefore when you meet Yuri the first time you will bring with you the current list of Air Force officers and enlisted personnel who will be scheduled at the time for transfer to the American forces in Austria. Put the list in an envelope and give it to Yuri. He will then give you your next assignment."

At the Vienna train station they got into a car and drove into the Soviet zone, stopping finally in front of the Central European Press Agency offices. Outside the car everyone shook hands with the American and bade him farewell.

The next day, as Ponger had said, Norrison was billeted aboard an Air Force DC-4 and flown back to Andrews Air Force Base in Maryland, just on the outskirts of Washington.

Three months later, on that balmy spring evening of Tuesday, April 12, 1951, he kept his appointment with Yuri at the base of the Washington Monument.

And now, in the shadows near the Washington momument, Herbert Norrison handed over the envelope with eight onionskin sheets of paper bearing the names of Air Force personnel leaving in the next few weeks for duty in Austria.

Yuri took the envelope and, without opening it to examine the contents, slipped it into the inside pocket of his jacket.

"The next thing we will want," Norrison's contact said in a thick Russian accent, "is information about the personnel stationed in the Military Intelligence Service headquarters in Washington. Get me a full report on all your fellow employees."

He directed Norrison to meet him again in a month, on the night of May 8, at Fan & Bill's Restaurant, a chop and steak house on Connecticut Avenue, directly opposite the Mayflower Hotel.

"Go in there at eight P.M. and order a drink. Tell the waiter you are expecting another person for dinner and wait until I arrive. We shall eat together—and I will take the information you bring at that time."

He then told Norrison to remain behind in the darkness for a few seconds until he had left. "Good-bye," Yuri called out as he strolled away toward the curb where a black, 1951 Cadillac limousine with diplomatic license plates had been parked with a chauffeur behind the wheel. Yuri got into the car and was driven away.

Norrison didn't know anything about his contact other than the name "Yuri." Nor did the others who had watched the two men come together. But they soon would—as quickly as they had developed the infrared still and movie films that were taken of this clandestine meeting.

These other observers were the agents of the FBI who had been ordered to take over the surveillance of Herbert Norrison from the very minute of his arrival in the United States.

The tip about this encounter between the MIS man and the Russian, along with information relating to the attempt to expand the espionage apparatus in Vienna to United States soil, had been relayed to the FBI by American intelligence agents in Austria. They had been watching the entire operation since its inception in February, 1949, when Kurt Ponger was enlisted by Vladimir.

And Herbert Norrison, who had so impressed the Soviets that they had paid him a special two-thousand-dollar bonus before his departure for the States—was actually a counterspy!

As a matter of record, after Ponger had approached Norrison early in June, 1949, the MIS man reported the incident that very day to his superiors. Norrison was questioned by MIS investigative agents, already aware of Ponger's and Verber's involvement with the Soviets.

"I didn't refuse," Norrison had told his interrogators, showing his ability to meet a crisis with intelligence. Although his training in MIS had never taken him into the field as an agent, he was alert to the move he had to make—and made it well. He had told Ponger, "Let me think it over."

The intelligence agents asked Norrison if he were willing to play along with the spy ring. It was a big break for the American side because until then no direct proof had been developed to link Ponger and Verber with any effort to get information on the USFA.

Would he be willing to take on the role of a double-agent?

"Certainly," Norrison replied immediately. "You tell me what to do and I'll do it."

And from then on, without ever betraying his hand, Norrison acted out the part of the traitor perfectly. The documents he had delivered into the hands of the Soviet agents had all been carefully doctored by MIS agents. Yet the Russians were fooled so completely they had paid him thirty-five hundred dollars.

Now, with Norrison in Washington, they were willing to pay additional sums for information that would continue to be just as valueless.

For example, the officer and enlisted personnel list that Norrison had delivered to Novikov at the Washington Monument was made up of the names of airmen assigned to the Air Force Band and to recruiting duty around the country.

His delivery of that list was the first of a total of twelve transmissions of supposedly confidential MIS and USFA documents over the next eleven months, lasting through March, 1952.

During that time, Norrison and Novikov went on to meet in a multitude of locations in Washington and its environs, invariably after dusk and seldom in the same place. Their encounters usually began with dinner, as at Fan & Bill's that night of May 8.

Norrison readily saw why Yuri liked to meet in restaurants. He was a huge man who sported an insatiable appetite. Novikov's menu at their second meeting consisted of the following: tomato juice, a dozen cherrystone clams, soup, salad with dressing (Russian, of course), a plank steak (with heaps of mashed potatoes and vegetables), three bottles of beer, cheese and crackers, apple pie à la mode, four cups of coffee, and three afterdinner cordials—not to mention two vodka martinis before the meal.

It was eleven thirty P.M. when Novikov paid the check, disgorged himself from the table, and escorted Norrison by the arm out to the sidewalk. Novikov chatted briefly outside the restaurant, mainly reiterating the time and place of their next meeting which had been arranged at the table. Also during dinner, Norrison had discreetly slipped the Russian another white envelope containing the list of employees at MIS headquarters in Washington which Novikov had asked for.

While they stood in front of the restaurant, FBI movie cameras positioned in a third-floor window of the Mayflower Hotel ground away more telltale footage of Novikov's espionage activity.

So it went over the next ten months, with meetings on a monthly basis.

On two occasions, Novikov's wife, Helen, accompanied her husband to encounters with Norrison in Washington restaurants. The three of them dined together like social acquaintances of long standing. And like her husband, Mrs. Novikov had a ravenous appetite and mirrored its consequences in her roly-poly figure.

In all, a total of nine Soviets—besides Yuri Novikov and his wife

—were observed and identified by the FBI in activity linked to the operation authorities called "the Hands-Across-the-Sea Spy Case," during the eleven months it functioned. Some of the Russians participated in the meetings between Novikov and Norrison, but primarily they acted as "secondaries" or "lookouts," whose job it was to observe whether the man from their Embassy and his American source were being followed by the FBI.

One mid-August meeting that had been arranged for Harvey's Restaurant on Connecticut Avenue was terminated abruptly at the very beginning by Novikov. As he was approaching the restaurant, Novikov spotted a Capital City motorcycle patrolman making his customary round of the street. The policeman had stopped his bike in front of Harvey's and gone inside to answer a call of nature. The sight of the policeman entering the restaurant was too much for Novikov. He turned on his heel, went back to the car he had parked up the block on Connecticut Avenue, and returned to the Embassy on 16th Street. From there he phoned Harvey's, had Norrison paged, and told him what had happened. He made a date with Norrison for the next night at another restaurant.

Then, suddenly, in March, 1952, Novikov cut himself off completely from Norrison without explanation. The FBI was baffled and it could only try to guess at the reason. Perhaps the Russians had finally found that the data they were getting were phony and realized they had been taken for an $8,550 sleighride.

Because they could not be certain Novikov hadn't made his last move, the FBI decided to play a waiting game. The Soviets might still come back to Norrison—or conceivably they might have found someone else in the Pentagon to do the dirty work for them, someone the FBI hadn't spotted yet. To expose the espionage ring at this time could readily spoil any chance the G-men had of detecting a new Soviet spy in the Pentagon, if indeed there was one.

So Novikov and the other Russians from the Embassy were kept under close surveillance for the balance of the year. But they didn't appear to get involved in any further schemes, and when it began to seem that all Soviet interest in the USFA had ceased on this side of the Atlantic, a decision was reached by the Justice Department to pull the rug from under the conspirators.

One of the motivating factors was the undiminished espionage activity by Verber and Ponger in Austria. Both men continued to supply Moscow with information about American military activity and other essential data. Verber, for example, made what use he could of casual USFA contacts in Vienna, unwitting sources, to keep him abreast of military developments and moves. Ponger, meanwhile, used his Central European Press Agency as a front to gather data about Austrian political developments, profiles on that country's political leaders, the status of Austrian Communists, the course of Austrian-U.S. relations, and the political attitudes and views of Slavic minority groups in Austria.

Quietly and without any public announcement in early December, 1952, the Justice Department began presenting evidence to a Federal grand jury in the capital. During the course of this investigation fourteen witnesses—most of them Air Force and Army Intelligence agents—as well as FBI men who had trailed Novikov and Norrison in Washington, testified about the conspiracy.

The grand jury finally returned sealed indictments against Verber and Ponger in early January, 1953, in which it charged fourteen overt acts of espionage. Novikov was named as co-conspirator but not a defendant because of his diplomatic status which gave him immunity from prosecution.

U.S. Army Intelligence in Austria was notified immediately of the jury's action and directed to take Verber and Ponger in custody. At the same time they were instructed to round up for questioning a number of others, including Walter Lauber, members of the accused men's families, and some U.S. Government employees in Vienna, including a man identified as Ernest Tislowitz, who worked for the U.S. Army in the Austrian capital.

The Army's agents had to be careful that they made the arrests in the American sector. But that was no problem. Careful observation of Verber and Ponger, and the others, had been going on for so long that the Army agents knew precisely when the suspects would be in the Western sector.

Ponger, for example, who lived in the Soviet zone, was in the habit of leaving there each morning to bring his seven-year-old daughter to school in the Western sector. Agents lay in wait and when he crossed over at ten thirty on the morning of Wednesday, January 14, they seized him; the daughter was placed in custody of Ponger's lawyer, who was also his father-in-law.

Fifteen minutes later, a counterintelligence detail entered Verber's house in the American sector of the city and arrested him as he sat at a typewriter pounding out a report on the USFA for transmittal to his Soviet espionage contacts. The paper was confiscated as evidence.

Almost at the same time other agents grabbed Lauber. He had been spotted earlier that morning dropping in at Ponger's house, then leaving together with a well-known Communist. While one team of Army men waited to follow Ponger and his school-bound daughter, another took off after Lauber. They followed him in his car as he drove with the Communist to the Postgrasse in Vienna's international zone. When he stopped to let his companion out, the agents seized Lauber. It was perfectly legal—this was the month the Americans had jurisdiction in the zone.

Mrs. Verber also was taken in for questioning, then released. She couldn't believe the charges against her husband and vowed to come to the United States and help him in his defense. By contrast, Mrs. Ponger was nowhere to be found. Immediately rumors abounded that she had taken refuge in Moscow.

The case created a sensation in Austria—not so much because of the arrests but because one of those seized was Mrs. Theresa Harris, the daughter of the city councillor, Rudolph Holzer. Her parents protested her detention at once. They said their daughter was so far from being a Communist that she didn't even know the meaning of Communism. Her father appealed to Chancellor Leopold Figl on grounds that American forces had no authority to seize a British subject on Austrian soil.

Nevertheless, Mrs. Harris was questioned for several hours before finally being released, along with Lauber and the others, after all had agreed to serve as material witnesses.

Before the day was out, Ponger and Verber were taken in handcuffs by Army agents, bundled aboard a C-54 military transport, and started back to the United States.

It was one A.M. on Friday, the 16th, when the giant airliner touched down at National Airport in Washington. Customs, Immigration, and FBI agents were waiting. They boarded the plane when it stopped in front of the military terminal.

The arrival also was recorded by a number of reporters and photographers; by now the story of the first case of espionage leading directly to the Soviet Embassy in Washington had made headlines across the nation. The news broke with the indictments, coupled with the Government's request to the Soviet Union to have Novikov sent back to Moscow.

Only twice before that time in the United States had Soviet officials been involved in illegal activity.

The first case, in 1948, implicated Jacob Lomakin, Soviet Consul-General in New York, in a plot by Soviet agents to kidnap Mme. Ilsana Kosenkina, a teacher at a Russian school conducted by the Soviet Consulate in New York; Mrs. Kosenkina had leaped from a window while being kept a prisoner in the Consulate.

The other case, in 1949, involved Valentin Gubitchev, Third Secretary of the Soviet Delegation to the United Nations, in New York, who was accused of conspiring with Justice Department employee Judith Coplon to steal, among other things, highly confidential files of FBI reports on the Red conspiracy in the United States.

Lomakin, who enjoyed diplomatic immunity, was declared persona non grata and returned to Moscow; Gubitchev, who had no diplomatic status, stood trial with Judith Coplon, was convicted, and sentenced to fifteen years. But he accepted the court's alternative—leave the United States and never return.

In Novikov's case, it had to be persona non grata treatment. He had diplomatic immunity. Even before Ponger and Verber had landed in Washington, the State Department made its formal appeal to the Soviet Embassy in Washington to expel Novikov. The note read:

"The Secretary of State presents his compliments to His Excellency, the Ambassador of the Union of Soviet Socialist Republics, and states the following:

" 'The Government of the United States has ascertained that Yuri V. Novikov, Second Secretary of the Embassy, has engaged in activities incompatible with his status as an accredited diplomatic official.

" 'Therefore, this Government is impelled to declare Mr. Novikov persona non grata. The Embassy is requested to make arrangements for his immediate departure from the United States.' "

At National Airport, fifteen minutes after FBI agents boarded the plane, a G-man emerged, followed by Verber, rumpled, hatless, and tieless. He was handcuffed to the agent. They ran down the ramp amid the flash of photographers' bulbs and scooted across the apron to a car parked nearby.

"Are you a spy?" a reporter shouted at Verber as he was being hustled into the car.

"No, sir," he snapped over his shoulder.

Moments later, a second agent came out of the plane with Ponger shackled to him and appearing as disheveled as Verber. It was another dash to the car, but Ponger ignored reporters' questions.

They were driven to the offices of U.S. Commissioner C. S. Lawrence for preliminary arraignment. In general the charges involved a conspiracy with Novikov to violate the Espionage Statutes; Verber and Ponger were accused of obtaining information relating to the intelligence and counterintelligence work of the Army and Air Force, and data relating to aircraft, defense works, and other military installations and operations.

According to the indictment, each overt act was committed "with intent and reason to believe that it would be used to the injury of the United States and to the advantage of Soviet Russia."

Commissioner Lawrence set bail at fifty thousand dollars each and ordered the prisoners remanded to the Federal House of Detention.

Meanwhile, word came from Vienna that Walter Lauber's Austrian-born wife, Cecilia, had fled with their two children, John, four, and Katherine Susanne, two, to the Soviet sector even as her husband continued under interrogation in the jail at United States headquarters in Salzburg.

Held along with him was Ernest Tislowitz, who had also been gathered up in the net thrown out for Verber and Ponger.

And authorities were still questioning Verber's wife and his father, Jack Verber.

"They are not being detained," explained an American official in Salzburg. "They were asked if they would voluntarily answer some questions and they agreed to do so."

Mrs. Verber, bordering on tears, still maintained that her husband couldn't have been involved in espionage. "I'm fully convinced of my husband's innocence," she persisted.

Back in Washington, Verber and Ponger were formally arraigned before Judge Alexander Holtzoff in Federal District Court in an air of mystery created by a Justice Department announcement that new indictments against Verber and Ponger might be returned as a result of further investigation into the case by the Government.

Although it wasn't stated publicly, the author has learned that

FBI and Army Intelligence agents had found evidence that Verber and Ponger were suspected of having been recruited by the Russians for espionage as far back as 1945, during the Nuremberg trials. Technically, the United States was then still at war with Japan. And the punishment for espionage during wartime could be death.

The new evidence showed Ponger and Verber had been associating closely with members of the Soviet ten-man prosecution staff in Nuremberg.

"Like some other members of the American staff, they eagerly chased after the Russians and were easy catches for the Red spy system," one U.S. official told the author.

Part of the evidence bore on charges of Communist influence in the Nuremberg trials that surfaced in 1949 when John J. McCloy, then High Commissioner in Frankfurt, was given legal briefs showing serious errors in translation from German and other languages into English. The errors, in some cases, were made by persons whose Communist ties had since been proved by loyalty checks.

Remember—both men had been decorated for their service on the commission; Ponger was credited in official U.S. Government reports of the trial with having rendered valuable assistance to the prosecution of Field Marshal Wilhelm von Leeb and thirteen other generals, as well as in the cases of Nazi Undersecretary of Foreign Affairs Ernst von Weizsaecker and twenty other members of Hitler's ministries; Verber received official recognition for his part in the von Weizsaecker trial.

Verber was represented in court by Walter J. Rockler, a Washington attorney, under whom he had worked as an interrogator at the Nuremberg trials. But Rockler told Judge Holtzoff he hoped he would not represent Verber at the trial. Ponger had no attorney and complained:

"There is no possibility of contacting anybody and I have no money to employ counsel."

Judge Holtzoff said he would appoint a lawyer for him.

Again the defendants were remanded to jail in default of the combined one-hundred-thousand-dollar bail that Holtzoff had previously set.

On that same day, Monday, January 19, the doors of the Soviet Embassy opened in Washington and a figure familiar to the FBI agents who had been on his trail emerged with his fur-trimmed coat collar turned up and black fedora angled down over his eyes. He hurried to a waiting limousine. A chauffeur was behind the wheel. In the back were a woman and a little girl.

The man was Yuri Novikov and the woman and girl were his wife, Klavdiya Vasilevna (also known as Helen), and their six-month-old daughter, Irina. They were on their way to National Airport for a shuttle flight to New York's LaGuardia Airport.

Novikov was going back to Moscow—persona non grata.

He eluded reporters in Washington, but the press in New York was more enterprising and managed to corner him between planes.

"Sorry, I'm not talking," he barked at newsmen as they surrounded him. But he dropped his belligerent mien a moment later and began smiling.

"Sure, I'm glad," he replied to a reporter who wanted to know if he was happy to leave the United States. "I'm glad to go back to my home country."

"Were you involved in espionage?" another newsman queried.

Novikov broke into a huge grin. "I won't say anything," he winked.

Moments later the ousted Russian emissary boarded a Sabena Belgian Air Lines plane with his wife and daughter, off for Prague, Czechoslovakia, en route to Moscow. With them went 300 pounds of baggage, including five bags of diplomatic mail. On the same plane, too, went Vladimir C. Polyakov, an attaché to the Soviet delegation to the U.N.—no doubt to insure Novikov's safe journey to Moscow.

Almost at the same time word came from Vienna that authorities had completed their interrogation of Lauber, after a nine-day detention, and had released him. He was joined by his wife, who returned to their home in the British sector in Vienna from the Soviet sector where the mystery of her whereabouts had finally been solved. She'd been staying with her parents.

A month later, the Communist newspaper *Volksstimme* in Vienna published a story that Lauber and his family had taken refuge in the Soviet sector and claimed that the ex-GI had told one of its reporters that the U.S. Counterintelligence Corps had subjected him to "Gestapo-type questioning."

According to *Volksstimme,* the U.S. Consulate had confiscated Lauber's passport and told him his ninety percent disability pension and GI Bill payments had been suspended.

That was the last heard of him.

Back in the United States, Ponger and Verber got themselves adequate legal representation and began what seemed like efforts to harass the prosecution. They mounted a defense motion to force public disclosure of the names of all Government employees whom the two men were accused of using in their espionage activities.

Government prosecutor William Hitz went before Judge Holtzoff and argued that disclosure of the contacts' names would endanger national security as well as their own safety. Ponger and Verber contended they couldn't prepare their defense unless they knew details of the charges against them in the sealed indictments.

Judge Holtzoff rejected the motions.

A plea for more time to prepare its case won the defense a postponement when court convened for the trial on March 2. The court put off the proceedings for April 13.

It was a minute after ten A.M. on the 13th when Judge Holtzoff rapped for order in the courtroom and prepared to begin the trial with selection of a jury.

All at once, attorney Roger Robb, who had been appointed by the court to represent Verber, stepped before the bench.

"Your Honor," Robb began. "I have informed my client of his legal rights. He fully understands them. And he wishes to inform the court that he wants to plead guilty."

Judge Holtzoff turned to Assistant U.S. Attorney William Hitz, who nodded affirmatively. Then the judge looked at Verber and asked if it was indeed his wish to plead guilty.

"That is correct," Verber muttered almost inaudibly.

"Do you admit the truth of the charge?" Holtzoff pressed.

"Yes, I do, your Honor," Verber replied in louder voice.

The Government then accepted Verber's plea of guilty to one count of espionage—carrying a maximum penalty of ten years in prison. Hitz agreed to dismiss the other charges—and made no mention of the additional indictments that had been hinted at previously and which could conceivably have resulted in the death penalty upon conviction.

Immediately speculation was touched off that Verber might have agreed to become a Government witness against his brother-in-law. But neither Hitz nor Oran H. Watterman, another Justice Department attorney, would say whether that was so.

Ponger's court-appointed counsel, James C. Toomey, let it be known after Verber was remanded to await sentencing that he intended to stand trial. Judge Holtzoff put it down on the calendar for the following day.

But when the case was called the next day and Ponger was lead with head bowed into the courtroom by U. S. marshals, the air of expectancy of a long, drawn-out trial evaporated the instant Assistant Prosecutor Hitz stepped before the bench.

"Your Honor," he said, "the defendant has informed the prosecution that he wishes to enter a plea of guilty to the first count of the indictment. The Government has no objection."

Judge Holtzoff glanced at Ponger, who was still hanging his head shamefacedly.

"Do you admit your guilt?" the court asked.

"Yes, I do, your Honor," Ponger replied quietly.

Judge Holtzoff then ordered the defendant remanded after stating that he would fix dates later for the sentencing of both Ponger and Verber.

Ponger pleaded guilty to a charge that could carry a possible death penalty. But Hitz explained to the court that the Government did not intend to offer any evidence that a technical state of war existed between the United States and Japan at the time of the spying activity. Such a showing was mandatory before the death penalty could be invoked.

As it stood, the maximum penalty for peacetime espionage was twenty years, which was what Ponger actually faced; Verber, could get only ten years because he had pleaded guilty to a lesser count in the indictment. The disparity of the charges hinged on the differentiation that Verber merely conspired to collect vital military secrets, while Ponger conspired to gather information on military intelligence and counterintelligence with intent to deliver the data to Russia.

On Monday, June 8, 1953, Ponger and Verber were again led into Judge Holtzoff's courtroom and stood grimly before the bench to hear their fate. Judge Holtzoff tempered mercy with justice as he decreed that Verber serve forty months to ten years and Ponger, five to fifteen years.

Verber was sent to the Federal Penitentiary at Lewisburg, Pennsylvania; Ponger to the one in Atlanta, Georgia.

A year and a week later, on June 14, 1954, Otto Verber's wife, Eva Marietta, walked into Supreme Court in Manhattan, accompanied by her father and an attorney, Nathaniel Ellenbogen, for a hearing before Referee Earle S. Warner. It was an annulment proceeding brought by Mrs. Verber, who was seeking to shed her husband on the grounds that he had made "fraudulent representation" by denying to her he was a member of the Communist Party before their marriage. The thirty-year-old Mrs. Verber also asked the court for custody of the two children, aged four and three years.

In her testimony, Mrs. Verber said that before her marriage on June 20, 1942, her father had suspicions about her fiancé's political affiliations. As a result, she had asked Verber whether he was a Communist. He denied it. On another occasion, in her father's house, she went on to say, Verber had Ponger with him and both again assured her Verber was not a Communist.

When her husband and Ponger were arrested and brought back to the United States, Mrs. Verber followed, visited Otto in jail in Washington, and asked him once more if he was a Communist. Verber, she testified, replied that he was, had been since 1938, and said he had concealed this fact from her because he knew she wouldn't have married him otherwise.

Mrs. Verber's father also took the stand and told essentially the same story, relating that he had begun to have misgivings about his daughter's husband long before their marriage, after Otto had given Eva a book espousing Communist ideology. The father said Verber reassured him he wasn't a Communist; yet when he saw his son-in-law after his arrest he admitted he had hidden his Communist affiliation because he knew he would never get permission to marry Eva.

Referee Warner reserved decision after the hearing, then convened court on June 23 to grant Mrs. Verber the annulment. It was a decision without precedent, the first to recognize concealment of Communist Party membership as a ground for annulment. It read:

"The husband had specifically represented prior to his marriage that he was not a Communist, that he did not believe in the doctrines of Communism, and that he was loyal to the United States. These representations were false and were made with the intention of deceiving the wife, who would not have married him had she known them to be false.

"Withholding this fact constitutes fraud and his denial was fraudulent representation."

The court also awarded Mrs. Verber custody of the two children, twenty dollars a week for their support, and permission to resume her maiden name.

Out of court, attorney Ellenbogen pleaded with reporters not to mention Mrs. Verber's maiden name in their stories. He explained that the children did not know about their father's conviction or imprisonment and believed that he was abroad. Mrs. Verber, he went on, was living in New York City and had a job and a future.

"They need a chance for a clean start in life," Ellenbogen declared.

As for Ponger's wife, reports indicated she had taken up residence with her children in the Soviet sector of Vienna to await her husband's return.

Nothing more was heard about Verber or Ponger for the next three years. Then on June 4, 1957, Verber's name again came up briefly when the Justice Department moved in New York's Federal Court to revoke his citizenship.

Judge John M. Cashin signed the judgment that stripped the traitor of his 1943 naturalization.

Three months later, on September 20, Federal Judge Edward Weinfeld was asked to take the same action against Ponger. Weinfeld granted the Justice Department's application which deprived Ponger of his citizenship.

The records show no further action taken against Lauber after he went to the Soviet sector of Vienna; nor was anything further done with Tislowitz or Theresa Harris. Although she had been turned over to British authorities because she was a British subject, prosecution was declined by the U.S. Government.

Otto Verber served six and a half years behind bars at Lewisburg (he earned three and a half years for good behavior) and was released to immigration authorities, who immediately brought him to New York and put him aboard an Austrian-bound airliner at International Airport. The flight took off at nine thirty P.M., February 23, 1960—and it was the last time Verber would see the United States.

Kurt Ponger served nine years of his maximum fifteen-year term, was released from Atlanta on September 19, 1962, and was deported to his native Austria in the same manner as Verber, by plane that left late at night on the 19th from International Airport in New York.

As of 1968, both Ponger and Verber were reportedly still in Austria—safely out of range of American military installations and personnel. Their days of spying against the United States are over.

4

The Embassy Spy Is Trapped by a Dead Man's Letter

"Our country, however bounded or described—still our country, to be cherished in all our hearts—to be defended by all our hands."

R. C. Winthrop was speaking of his country, the United States, when he wrote that passage. At the Soviet Embassy in Washington, they spout similar phrases, speaking about their country. The words are directed to those Russian expatriates the Kremlin would like to see return home. The Soviets have no legal power to force defectors back, but they are permitted to talk with them, as long as their methods of persuasion don't involve pursuit and harassment.

On October 26, 1956, Gennadi Fedorovich Mashkantsev and his wife Raisa Pavlovna Mashkantseva, arrived in Washington from Moscow and moved into an apartment house called the Woodner, on 16th Street—expensive surroundings for a couple living on the salary of a consulate employee in the Soviet Embassy.

Gennadi Mashkantsev's duties in the Embassy's consulate division had to do with repatriation of former Soviet citizens and defectors who might have had a change of heart about living in the United States and wanted to return to Mother Russia.

How well the stocky, blond-haired Mashkantsev performed his duties from the day he stepped into his post until the night of March 6, 1957, is something the FBI isn't prepared to say. But from all outward appearances he kept within the limits allowed because nobody complained to the authorities.

Then at eight-thirty that night the FBI got a call from a man who identified himself as Peter Pirogov. He said he was a former Soviet Air Force pilot who had defected to the United States in 1948, and had since been living happily in Alexandria.

In fact, he told the FBI on the phone, he liked America so much that he and his wife had just bought a home.

"We moved in only last Saturday," Pirogov said. "All week we worked to get the place ready, and tonight we had our first guests over. We were in the middle of dinner when we got a telephone call from the Soviet Embassy. A man who called himself Mashkantsev said he wanted to come over tonight to see me. I told him that was impossible because we had people at the house. I asked him to call back in a couple of days."

Then in a voice edged with fear, "I don't want to have any dealings with this man. What shall I do?"

Would Pirogov be willing to see some FBI agents this evening—after his guests went home?

"Yes, yes. Thank you so much. I will be waiting."

The FBI men were at Pirogov's home shortly after his visitors left at eleven-thirty P.M. The agents sat with him for fully an hour, first listening to the story of his defection from the Soviet Union, then advising him how to handle Mashkentsev should he call again —but urging him, above all, to keep the FBI informed of every move.

Pirogov's story was poignant; he had been a pilot in the Soviet

Air Force during World War II, was discharged after the fighting ended, went home, found conditions unbearable, and decided to flee his homeland. Together with another former Soviet flier named Anatoli Barzov, Pirogov fled across the border into Poland, then onward into West Germany. There he and Barzov parted. Pirogov emigrated to the United States; Barzov remained behind. But about a year later, the Soviet diplomatic corps tracked Barzov down, sold him a bill of goods, and made him return to the Soviet Union.

"I do not want what happened to Anatoli to happen to me," Pirogov told the FBI agents with terror in his voice. "You must protect me and my family. I do not want to go back to Russia. The United States is my country. I beg you to help me."

The G-men assured Pirogov he had nothing to worry about. They advised him to see Mashkantsev if he called again and find out what he was up to.

The next two days passed without a whisper from the Soviet diplomat. When the weekend went by and he still hadn't heard from him, Pirogov began to breathe a little easier.

But his air of false confidence dissolved abruptly at seven o'clock on the night of March 12, 1957, just after the family had sat down to dinner and the telephone rang.

It was Mashkantsev.

"Are you free to see me tonight?" he asked. "I have a big surprise for you that has just arrived from Russia."

"Yes," replied Pirogov with reluctance, "you may come over."

At eight fifteen P.M. the doorbell rang. Pirogov found a stocky, fair-skinned man of about thirty-five with light hair, blue eyes, and pleasant features standing on the stoop, smiling benevolently. He was wearing a dark blue topcoat and holding a gray fedora in his left hand.

"Petr," he said cheerfully.

Pirogov shook hands with the visitor wordlessly. His long face was gaunt with strain.

"Please come in," he said.

As he walked into the foyer of the two-story private dwelling, the Soviet diplomat glanced around the house with intense curiosity.

"You have a beautiful home," Mashkantsev said. "It must have cost you a fortune."

"Please let me have your coat," Pirogov said. Mashkantsev handed his hat and coat to his host who hung them in the closet, then showed him into the living room.

"Vodka?" asked Pirogov, feeling just a little more at ease after the initial contact with the Soviet diplomat.

"With pleasure," replied Mashkantsev. Pirogov headed to the kitchen, brought his wife into the living room, and introduced the visitor. Then he asked her to make some drinks.

Mashkentsev settled back in an armchair and talked about the "surprise" he'd promised to bring. He reached into his inside jacket pocket, pulled out an unsealed envelope containing a letter, and handed it to Pirogov.

Pirogov opened the letter.

What he read was a direct, handwritten appeal to him to return to Russia.

". . . It was very foolish of me to leave the Soviet Union," the message said after some warm introductory salutations and brief but not specific recollections of the "old days" in the Soviet Air Force. "But you were even more foolish than I to run away from Russia. I returned and found the only life that is worth living, while you have not. I am surprised that you have not yet seen your duty to come home to your land and to correct the harm that you are doing the country of your birth by staying in the United States. . . . I beg you to return . . ."

It was a long, rambling letter which went on extolling the virtues of the Soviet Union and the joys of living there. It was propaganda, pure and simple, as Pirogov quickly judged for himself.

As he came to the end, he glanced at the signature with close, troubled attention. It was that of his old friend Anatoli Barzov.

Pirogov looked at Mashkantsev who was fondling the drink Mrs. Pirogov had just brought.

"Is this really from Anatoli?"

Mashkantsev threw his head back and laughed. "Why do you act so surprised? Do you think I have brought you something counterfeit? Of course it is from Anatoli."

Pirogov handed the letter to his wife and turned to the consul.

"Tell me, Mr. Mashkantsev, did you see Anatoli yourself?"

"Of course," Mashkantsev said. "I saw him only last month, just before I left the Soviet Union for my duties in the Embassy here. Anatoli was one of the last persons I spoke to there. He is living in Moscow and, as you can see from what he has written, he is most happy."

For the next two hours, Mashkantsev mixed pleasant conversation with intense probing into many matters—Pirogov's financial state, his employment status, social contacts, and friends. But it was all part of the Soviet consul's grand design to establish a platform for appealing to Pirogov to return to the Soviet Union.

The plea came after Mashkantsev had held the Pirogovs fascinated with a picture of a pleasant, modern Russia.

"And by the way," he finally asked, "have you ever given any thought to returning to Russia yourselves?"

Although Pirogov had been anticipating the question all evening, he stiffened when it was posed.

"Too many things have happened since I came to America," Pirogov said. "If I were to consider any such proposal I would have to give it long and serious thought."

Mashkantsev peered at Pirogov. "You are probably thinking that you will be punished if you return to Russia. Is that why you hesitate to reply?"

"I do not know what to think," Pirogov said. "What did they do to Anatoli?"

"I must explain that when Anatoli returned in 1948, things were very different," Mashkantsev said. "You see, Premier Khrushchev has introduced many reforms, and one of those is that we do not punish expatriates who return to our country. It was different when Stalin was the leader."

Pirogov interrupted his visitor. "But you have not answered my question. What happened to Anatoli?"

"He went to prison . . . but he was finally released when the Premier declared an amnesty."

"How long was he in prison?"

"I think five years . . . but that has all been forgiven and Anatoli is living a free man today," Mashkantsev said with a wave of his hand.

"What is important, my friend," he added quickly, "is that you are welcome to go back without any punishment whatsoever. You will be received with gladness."

Mashkantsev smiled at Mrs. Pirogov.

"You see, I intend to contact the Soviet Ministry of Foreign Affairs in Moscow and have them send direct to you the assurance that you will not be punished."

He looked at his watch and stood up abruptly.

"Let me assure you," he said as Pirogov and his wife rose to escort him to the door, "that we will even provide some financial assistance to help you return to your motherland."

Pirogov retrieved the diplomat's hat and coat from the closet.

"I will think about what you have said," he promised. "But I will need time."

"I hope you will write a reply to Anatoli's letter," Mashkantsev said as he went out. "I shall be glad to send it to him through our Embassy. I shall be back in about a week for your letter . . ."

Pirogov watched Mashkantsev get into a car and drive away. Then he hurried to the phone and called the FBI at the number he had been given.

Only minutes passed before the doorbell rang. FBI agents had never been more than a hundred feet from the house during Mashkantsev's visit.

Pirogov told the agents everything Mashkantsev had said and showed the letter from Anatoli.

"Do you have any doubt that this is from your old friend?" one of the FBI men asked.

Pirogov grimaced. "Excuse me, please," he said, starting for the bedroom. He returned a minute later, another letter in hand. He gave it to the agent who was holding the letter the Soviet diplomat had brought.

"Look down here, please," Pirogov said, pointing to the signatures. "They look alike, no?" he asked.

The G-man nodded.

"But do you see this?" Pirogov put his finger on the second letter of the last name signed on the letter Mashkantsev had given him. Then he directed the agent's attention to the same place in the name signed to the letter he had brought from the bedroom, which has been written to Pirogov in 1948 before Barzov returned to Russia.

"See that?"

The name was spelled Barzov in the old letter, Borzov in the new.

The difference in the "o" and the "a" was barely perceptible.

"May we take these letters along?" asked the agent.

"Of course," Pirogov said.

"By the way," asked another agent, "was that what made you suspicious of the letter, or is there something else that makes you distrust Mashkantsev?"

"I could not really tell by the handwriting," Pirogov admitted. "The little difference in the signature would not make me suspicious. But I happen to know . . ."

He let his words drift off for a moment, perhaps to set the stage for the dramatic punch line he was about to deliver.

"You see . . . I know that Anatoli Barzov was executed."

Pirogov showed the G-men another letter from Russia. It was from a friend, who told of how Barzov was killed by a firing squad.

The test at the FBI laboratory established what Peter Pirogov suspected all along—the letter was a skillful forgery. It had been so expertly simulated to look like Barzov's handwriting that the only serious slip was in the signature. Otherwise, to the naked eye and even under microscopic examination, the script looked remarkably similar to the dead man's hand.

A week went by and Mashkantsev had not returned to see Pirogov as he'd promised. Pirogov was certain he would see the visitor again. He knew the Russians wouldn't give up on him.

Every night, Pirogov sat home with his wife waiting for the bell to ring. And it finally did.

It was eight-thirty on the night of March 26—just two weeks later—that Mashkantsev returned. He brought glad tidings—any day now the foreign ministry would grant Pirogov immunity to return to Russia.

"The Soviet Government also will pay all expenses necessary to transport you as well as your family back to the motherland," Mashkantsev informed Pirogov excitedly. "Is that not a wonderful offer?"

Pirogov said it was. Then he was told that Moscow had to be assured of one thing—that Pirogov was willing to sign a paper saying he wanted to return to Russia voluntarily. Mashkantsev just happened to have brought the application for repatriation with him. Did Pirogov want to sign it?

"No, no," Pirogov cried, "I have not reached a decision. I am not ready. I need more time to think."

"How long?" Mashkantsev demanded. "Keep in mind that if it isn't accepted by you very soon the ministry may withdraw its kind offer. Not everybody is treated so generously. Remember, you must come to a decision without any more delay."

Pirogov reiterated his earlier hesitation, that there was so much to consider.

"I have this house," he said, shifting uneasily in his chair. "I do not want to lose my life's savings I have invested in it."

"Do not worry," Mashkantsev said. "We can arrange for a quick sale, and you will get all your money back. If you suffer any loss in the transaction, we will make up the difference."

For the hour that Mashkantsev stayed, he did not relent a moment, returning again and again, each time more compellingly, to the urgency of a decision. Finally, he said:

"I will give you exactly one month from tonight to give me your answer. You must tell me then what you have decided."

With his ultimatum issued, Mashkantsev rose abruptly and left.

But in fact, the ultimatum applied to Mashkantsev and his wife.

The FBI submitted the evidence of its findings to the Justice Department which, in turn, presented them to the State Department. It was decided that Gennadi Fedorovich Mashkantsev, consulate officer in the Soviet Embassy, had used deceit (he lied about having come over from Moscow in February; he also lied when he said he saw Anatoli Barzov) and employed forgery (the letter) in trying to influence a former Soviet citizen to return to Russia.

He was declared persona non grata for his activities against Peter Pirogov.

At exactly three five P.M. on April 25, 1957, Mashkantsev and his wife boarded a Scandinavian Airlines plane at New York's International Airport, which with ensuing spy cases would become the most popular jumping-off point in the United States for departing discredited diplomats bound for Moscow.

Unlike other Soviet diplomats who engaged in espionage and got caught, Gennadi Fedorovich Mashkantsev was caught not as a spy, but for a lie. He had been trapped by a dead man's letter.

5

The Washington Correspondent and the
Soviet Stocking Dodge

Washington correspondent!—the name thrums with action, drama, power. The Washington press corps! The excitement of Presidential press conferences, of private briefings with the Secretary of State, of diplomatic receptions.

However, this glamor actually characterizes only a handful of lives, perhaps two dozen stars of the press. For the thousands of others, most especially for the free-lancers like Charles Beaumet, who try to make their living reporting the day-in and day-out happenings of the most complicated, most complex, most bureaucratic, evasive, cautious, and occasionally downright boring information center on earth, Washington has all the thrill and excitement Nebraska cornfield.

Consider Charles Beaumet's condition during those gripping, turbulent months of late summer and early autumn, 1956. The British were preparing their historic and ill-fated invasion of Suez,

Soviet Russia's massive war machine was already cranking up to crush the Hungarian rebellion, and President Dwight D. Eisenhower was facing a determined, indefatigable Adlai Stevenson in a grueling campaign that would be settled in a landslide for Ike a few weeks later. Amid all that tumultuous history-in-the-making, Charlie Beaumet, reporter, was trooping about Washington researching an article—of all things—on the hosiery industry in Russia! And since one way to learn about this industry was by asking the Russians themselves, Charles Beaumet went to the Soviet Embassy.

The Embassy people greeted Beaumet cordially. If they were amused at the somewhat sad-faced young journalist, they kept it to themselves.

After passing from receptionist to secretary to a perplexed young fourth attaché, Beaumet found himself seated in the rather drably furnished cubicle of one Nikolai Ivanovich Kurochkin, Third Secretary of the Soviet Embassy in charge of, among other things, "press matters."

Beaumet explained the nature of his visit and submitted a list of questions. Kurochkin studied them and said in reasonably good English, "Well, it will take time to give you the answers. If I can have a week . . ."

Certainly, Beaumet said. "Naturally I'd like the information as quickly as possible . . ."

"A week," Kurochkin assured him. "Come back in a week."

The following week, Kurochkin still didn't have the information, but insisted it would now be only a matter of days. Beaumet sighed, shrugged, and waited. And waited. And waited.

By the middle of October, the information was still unavailable and Beaumet was ready to call the whole frustrating assignment off, when Kurochkin unexpectedly invited him to a reception at the Soviet Embassy. The reception actually was to promote the Russian magazine *USSR,* but possibly out of some feeling of guilt or neglect, Charlie Beaumet was urged to attend.

"My apologies, my friend," Kurochkin smiled at Beaumet over the punch bowl. "You must be impatient, I know. But all those production figures, statistics, forecasts—my friend, it takes time. And who can say what women want in styles; not even the women can agree, eh?"

Beaumet delivered the required smile and sipped his punch.

"Believe me," Kurochkin continued, "I want to cooperate. I have sent five, maybe six urgent letters to the proper ministry in Moscow."

He gave Beaumet a knowing nudge. "But we know how government agencies work, eh?" He lifted his eyes to the ceiling and shook his head. "Impossible."

And so on. Kurochkin appeared genuinely concerned about Beaumet's assignment and vowed to do more to get the information for him. The Russian, a pleasant, dark-haired man of five feet eight and a stocky 180 pounds, was jovial throughout the reception and told of his own journalistic experiences in Russia.

He had studied journalism at the University of Moscow and had worked on several small newspapers in the Soviet hinterlands before joining the diplomatic corps. He liked diplomacy well enough, but he occasionally missed the satisfaction of deadline newspapering. He had come to the United States only the previous April 4, and his duties were, in fact, to keep the American public informed, through the American press, of the Russian way of life in order to improve relations between the two countries.

As a journalist himself, therefore, Kurochkin told Beaumet, "I sympathize with your impatience at these irritating delays. But I'll make up for it. There is much to write about Russia, and I will help you with other articles."

This was fine, except that the deadline for the hosiery article was closing in, and Beaumet found himself pressing the Soviet Embassy. When, in spite of his prodding, it appeared he wouldn't get the material, Charlie Beaumet considered dropping the assignment entirely, and in the process reassessed his career as a free-lance writer.

It wasn't only the trouble he'd been having with the Soviets that disturbed him. The whole problem of scrounging around for material, of talking to third assistant assistants everywhere he went, the nagging sense of loss at missing the big stories of the day, all eroded his free-wheeling independence, and in the end Charlie Beaumet decided to join a payroll.

It was November, 1956, when he signed on as Pentagon correspondent for the National Guard Association's magazine, *The National Guardsman*. It wasn't daily journalism in the tradition of *The New York Times* or even the *Port Chester Daily Item,* but it was steady work and it was in the Pentagon where a lot of the really big decisions were being made.

In the press of his new duties, Beaumet almost forgot the Soviet hosiery article, and thus it came as something of a surprise when, in mid-November, Nikolai Ivanovitch Kurochkin phoned him at home and told him he had the material in his office.

During his lunch break next day, Beaumet went to the Soviet Embassy. Kurochkin was effusive in his apologies for taking so long.

"That's all right, forget it," Beaumet said. "It isn't so crucial anymore." He smiled. "I have a steady job."

"Ah? So. That is fine. Are you with the great *New York Times,* a bright enterprising young man like you?"

"No," Charlie Beaumet said ruefully, *"The National Guardsman.* It's the National Guard Association's magazine. The National Guard is—"

Kurochkin held up his hand and smiled benevolently. "I know about the National Guard. Don't you know that all Russians know everything about your military?"

He laughed. Beaumet smiled.

"Well, thanks for the material," Beaumet said, tucking it under his arm. "If I have any problems writing it, I'll call you."

"Feel free to," Kurochkin returned. He rose from his desk and escorted Beaumet to the door. "What sort of stories do you write for *The National Guardsman?*" he asked casually. "Surely not about the stocking industry in Russia?"

"No, I'm covering the Pentagon."

"Well, then," Kurochkin replied, "you'll find your work a bit more interesting. Congratulations."

"Thanks," Beaumet said. "I only hope I don't run into too much red tape." He ran a hand over the hosiery information under his arm. "Another story like this and I'd go out of my mind."

"I'm sure you'll do well," Kurochkin said. "I have enjoyed your friendship. I hope it won't end now. Possibly we can have lunch together soon."

Beaumet agreed and left. He wrote the hosiery article, did other free-lance work, went about his daily job of covering the Pentagon, and thus spent a busy fall, winter and spring.

Nonetheless he was as far away from that big jackpot story as ever. True, he was covering the Pentagon, but the Pentagon is a thousand different things to a thousand different people, and his work for *The National Guardsman,* while occasionally stimulating, was really no different from, for example, covering the Pentagon for the National Office Workers Association.

And so Charles Beaumet plodded along, biding his time, looking for the Big Story—and all the while growing more and more distant in time and memory from Nikolai Ivanovich Kurochkin whom he hadn't seen or talked to for some eight months.

When Kurochkin did call, then, on July 14, 1957, it came as a distinct surprise to Beaumet. The call was to his home.

"Greetings, my friend," said the barely familiar voice. "I have been thinking about you."

Beaumet mumbled some appropriate words and Kurochkin responded in kind. Then came the invitation to lunch. "A little late," said the Russian, "but I have not forgotten that I suggested it at our last meeting."

They agreed on a date—August 2—and the two men met for dinner instead of lunch at a restaurant on North Glebe Road in Arlington, a favorite spot for the diplomatic corps in Washington.

Kurochkin was, as always, spirited in conversation and thoroughly entertaining. They ordered vodka, and the Russian rhapsodized about the national drink, describing in detail the way it is distilled, the differences between Russian and American vodka, and the differences among the American brands alone. Naturally enough (he was, after all, a diplomat), the American brands were not inferior to Russian vodka, "just different."

The dinner was pleasant. Kurochkin moved from vodka as a subject to his impressions of the United States ("a rich, comfortable country, but you have had one hundred and seventy-five years since your revolution"), to an account of his childhood in his native Tamboc, to some homey anecdotes about his wife, Liliya, to his career as a diplomat and, by extension, to his former career as a journalist.

"You know," he said, "I still do an occasional article for the Soviet press. The money helps, but I believe the real reason is that once you are a journalist—you like to use the term 'newspaperman' but in my country it is always 'journalist'—once you are a journalist, you never cease being one. You understand, eh, my friend? The writer in us never dies. Anyway, I haven't done an article for several months and I would like to resume again. You could help me. I have very few American friends and any information or ideas I could get from the friends I do have would help greatly. You write for the National Guard. Perhaps I could do a piece on the military, perhaps something amusing. I am said to have a light touch."

"Well, sure, I suppose so," said Beaumet. "What did you have in mind?"

"Oh, nothing special. I thought possibly an article on Army basic training in the United States as contrasted to basic training in the Soviet Union. I think the Soviet people would find it interesting.

There would seem also to be room for humor in it. The plight of the young recruit during his first few weeks in the Army is a subject of much humor in my country and, I believe, in yours. Perhaps you could direct me to some material on the subject?"

"Sure. There's a ton of material on basic training . . ."

Charles Beaumet reflected a moment. The thought of espionage flashed through his mind, but the request for easily available information about Army basic training was surely innocent, and the article did, in fact, sound like a pretty good one. He wished he had thought of it.

"I'll pick some of it up tomorrow and drop it off to you."

Beaumet dispatched the material, and ten days later Kurochkin phoned and announced happily that he had sold the article to a Moscow magazine.

"Four hundred rubles," he trilled. "A little more than four hundred dollars. And for you, my friend—half!"

Beaumet was startled. He'd done nothing but mail off a few pamphlets. "No, I couldn't," he said.

"Yes, absolutely," Kurochkin said. "I couldn't have written the article without your help and it would not be right if I didn't pay it. Please, you must accept it."

"But I didn't pay you for the help you gave me," Beaumet protested.

"That was different," said the Russian. "I was simply carrying out my diplomatic function. This is as one journalist to another. It is a professional obligation on my part."

Beaumet hesitated. "Well, all right then, if you put it on a professional basis."

"Fine," Kurochkin said. "You see? It is a profitable partnership. Let us have dinner together and we will talk about more articles."

They met again four days later, and then two days after that. Each time, Kurochkin picked up the tab. To reciprocate, young Beaumet had Kurochkin and his wife to his own apartment for dinner. During the course of their socializing, both men learned of their common interest in hunting, and on three successive weekends, they trooped out in the hazy red-gray dawn to the fox-and-partridge country south of Alexandria, for bird-shooting.

Both in the fields and over dinner in the several restaurants they visited, Kurochkin reiterated the theme of their profitable partnership. He sold another, than a third, and then a fourth article, all based on contrasts between Soviet and American military men, weapons, or training procedures.

Several times, Beaumet asked to see the articles, but Kurochkin each time brushed the request aside, saying either that they were not yet in print or that they were in Russian and hence incomprehensible to Beaumet. All the articles were about nonsensitive subjects. Beaumet's only contribution was supplying the appropriate handouts, brochures, or other information that was always available to anyone interested enough in writing to the Government . . . except for several requests for such information as the latest in tank equipment, the latest in bombsight designs, the latest in submarine capabilities.

The questions were put innocently enough by Kurochkin each time, and Beaumet's answers were dutifully negative. But gradually, Kurochkin seemed to increase his requests for classified information, and also to become more generous in his payments to Beaumet.

Kurochkin alternated between sweetness, particularly when he reminded Beaumet of their "partnership," and almost downright belligerency when he insisted he couldn't write an article without a particular bit of information (the altitude capabilities of a certain experimental jet fighter, for example, or the intricacies of a computer used as a firing guide aboard specified U.S. Navy vessels)—information about computers of such sophistication that as each round was fired, they took into account the speed of the earth's revolution and the fact that a fraction of an inch of steel measured in the thousandths had been worn away from the cannon bore by the previous shell.

All such data were routinely denied by Beaumet, and usually lamented gracefully by Kurochkin.

For more than six months, the "partnership" continued, but the Russian diplomat became increasingly persistent, and by early June, 1958, Beaumet was satisfied that there was nothing at all innocent about his Soviet colleague's inquiries.

And finally, on June 3, he made the phone call he had suspected he would have to make all along. He called the FBI and said, in effect, "He's yours."

For what Charlie Beaumet had done long ago, on the very first day that Nikolai Ivanovitch Kurochkin had asked him for military information, was to call the FBI and then subsequently call them each time he met the Russian.

He gave the Bureau full details of every bit of information Kurochkin requested and filled them in about all their conversations. And for most of that period, of course, Kurochkin was under the constant surveillance of FBI agents. There was very little the G-men didn't know about the Soviet Embassy's Third Secretary.

Now, on June 3, Beaumet was calling the FBI again, and informing them that Kurochkin had offered to pay a substantial sum for some highly classified material. There was no pretense of innocence. It was out-and-out espionage.

That was enough for the FBI. They turned over all their information to the State Department, and on June 6, 1958, Nikolai Ivanovitch Kurochkin was declared persona non grata. Five days later, Kurochkin, the easygoing, entertaining Russian, left the United States with his family, under the watchful eyes of a dozen FBI agents.

Shortly before his departure, he contacted Beaumet and rather pathetically scolded him. "You didn't tell me you were doing this to me."

"Well," said Beaumet sternly, "there were a lot of things you didn't tell me, either. You underestimated us, Nikolai, a sad mistake."

6

A Washington Spy Courts the Quakers

It is a United States postulate, adequately supported by history, that virtually all foreign embassies on its soil are involved in intelligence work. The air attaché for a nation is assumed to be busy accumulating information about America's air potentialities, about its current experimental work, about its aircraft manufacturing orders. The naval attaché for even our staunchest ally, while he is attending assorted protocol lunches and perhaps even helping devise a common naval defense posture, is nevertheless known by the United States Government to be sniffing out classified information he feels his own government might find useful.

In general, all nations tolerate the intelligence activities of guests, if they are friendly or neutral to the host, for two reasons:

First, a friendly or neutral nation is not likely to use the clandestine information, however important it may be, in a hostile way.

Second, ousting a friendly foreign diplomat because he's been caught at some navy yard with a camera would impute a dangerous motive to the diplomat's government, result in a series of charges and countercharges that would be embarrassing to both nations, and place a strain on relations that could conceivably end in a diplomatic rupture neither side wanted.

However, in the case of the Iron Curtain countries and most particularly the Soviet Union, the rules of the game are radically altered. The signatories of the Warsaw Pact, forged by the Eastern European bloc just after World War II as a military response to NATO, and led then as now by Russia, are acknowledged by Washington as "nonfriendly" nations. And where allied and neutral nations persist in accumulating intelligence information while regarding maintenance of sound diplomatic relations as the *primary* purpose of their consuls and embassies in the United States, "nonfriendly" nations regard the accumulation of intelligence information as *their* primary purpose.

For that reason, the espionage efforts of Iron Curtain countries are considerably more intensive. Perhaps no better example of this exists than the so-called wave technique.

An ocean wave breaks upon the shore, accomplishes its erosion, and retreats back into the sea. Yet even while it is pounding the seacoast and before it returns as undertow, the ocean is already sending in another wave. There is, of course, an overlap, a brief time when the retreating and new wave occupy the same space.

So it was in the summer and autumn of 1957, the following winter, and the spring of 1958 when, as we have seen, Nikolai Ivanovitch Kurochkin was cleverly trying to dupe reporter Charles Beaumet into supplying classified information. Already the Kremlin was studiously preparing its follow-up "wave"—in the person of Eugeni Alekseevich Zaostrovtsev.

Zaostrovtsev, a plump, almost cherubic-looking man with brown hair and cool gray eyes, arrived in Washington on August 2, 1957, accompanied by his pretty wife, Ella, and their eleven-month-old son, Yuri. Zaostrovtsev was twenty-eight, his wife twenty-one. To the casual eye, they appeared to be a commonplace tourist family, possibly from Iowa, well-fed and ruddy from the sun.

If they had any thoughts of sightseeing though, they had to put them aside for the time being. Zaostrovtsev's destination was the Soviet Embassy and he went there directly from the train station while his wife and child went to the hotel suite the Russians had reserved for them.

Eugeni Alekseevich Zaostrovtsev, like Kurochkin, was not a specialist in any field. He belonged to that school of Soviet espionage agents upon whom the mother country relies for the assimilation of policy trends; not for the innovations in, for example, America's antimissile development program, but for the development of America's thinking, however vague or disjointed, on the troop withdrawal question in West Germany.

Zaostrovtsev's training and background was in the humanities, in economics, literature, philosophy, history, languages.

The assignment he received then, on reporting to the Embassy, was to establish as many contacts in the cultural field as he could. As a cover, the Russians provided him with an appropriate background: he would be the Cultural Attaché for Cinema and Education.

Ostensibly he would speak before American art groups on the state of the cinema in Russia, act as adviser to American filmmakers on Soviet life, provide information to the American press on his own country's educational methods, meet with American educators for advanced discussions on Soviet-American student, teacher, and other cultural exchanges. He would, to every extent possible, circulate among the intellectual leaders in the nation's capital.

Covertly, he would pick the brains of the American intellectual community, watch for signals to changes in U.S. policies, piece together random bits of information that might point to a trend, but above all remain close to the opinion-makers and opinion-reflectors in Washington, particularly if they were high in the Government.

It was a broad assignment, and its success depended on Zaostrovtsev's ability to establish rapport with his intended informers.

Even as Kurochkin was trying to win information from Charles Beaumet in that summer of 1957, Eugeni Alekseevich Zaostrovtsev was busy laying the groundwork for his own espionage activities and doing it in as blandly acceptable a fashion as its nature dictated. Slowly, innocuously, he began corresponding with various cultural groups in the United States. Employing contacts previously made by the Soviet Embassy, he sent out brochures to theater organizations, cinematic art groups, drama clubs, and professorial associations, particularly those with a known leftist orientation.

He also sought out various groups with histories of peace and nonviolence. Some were ad hoc committees formed specifically, for example, "to ban the bomb," to call for the withdrawal of American troops in Europe and Asia, or dismantle America's nuclear installations in Spain, Scandinavia, Turkey. They were neither subversive nor Communist-fronted, but their opposition to United States military preparedness made them potentially valuable, though unwitting, allies to the Soviet cause.

In particular, Zaostrovtsev tried to establish cordial relations with the Society of Friends, better known as the Quakers, a venerable, religious body that traces its beginnings to 1647 in England, and that was brought to the American colonies in 1656. The Quakers have gained an honorable place in every culture in which they have existed, and in many cases have brought significant progress in law, human rights, philosophy, and in the entire social fabric. Their gains have been all the more remarkable because they have been achieved not by militant lobbying, but through passiveness.

It was precisely that passiveness, the resistance Quakers had shown to all forms of warfare, that Eugeni Zaostrovtsev hoped to translate into espionage gains for the Soviet Union.

Accordingly, he helped sponsor a project that superficially, at least, fitted into the Quakers' historic efforts at spreading peace by reducing tensions wherever they arose. Working with the Quakers in Washington and with the Young Friends Committee of North America, a Quaker-sponsored organization, Zaostrovtsev helped arrange a program that brought several Soviet youths as guests to the United States in early 1958.

The ostensible purpose was simply to increase each young group's knowledge of the other, to let the Russian youths see and learn about America, and to allow American youths to meet and understand Soviet young people.

To the extent that it met that goal, it must be said, fairly, that the program succeeded.

But behind it lay of course, Eugeni Zaostrovtsev's scheme to utilize the Quakers for his own purposes; here, to meet the several Government employees Zaostrovtsev knew from a study of Russia's massive files on Washington belonged to Quaker organizations.

Among them was a twenty-eight-year-old State Department officer whose name will be rendered here as Frank Harrison.

Harrison was active in the Soviet youth program, though in an unofficial capacity. Zaostrovtsev didn't single Harrison out from among other Government workers, but a rapport was established between them based on Harrison's lively interest in Soviet society.

They met at first only in the company of others, but after a decent interval Zaostrovtsev suggested they meet alone, saying, "Your friends don't share your interest in Soviet living; they seemed to be bored at the way we monopolized the conversation."

The State Department employee agreed, and the two met in an expensive restaurant on Connecticut Avenue where the Russian dined on sirloin steak and the American on Rock Cornish hen.

That particular detail comes from Harrison's diary. Harrison was an inveterate diarist, and some of the entries he made of his encounters with Eugeni Zaostrovtsev have been made available. Some, for security reasons, have not.

One entry, dated May 17, 1958, says in part:

"Fifteen of us, including five from the Soviet youth group, took tour of Soviet Embassy. Everyone cordial enough, but restrained. Large rooms, but not as elegant as other embassies I've seen. Interesting tour. Then we watched movie on Soviet farm life with Americans later asking questions of Soviet students and several Embassy aides. Z [for Zaostrovtsev] acted as interpreter. Gathering broke up and Z took me aside and said he wanted to do a paper on the Quakers. Apparently he's done some writing and wants to sell an article. Told him I thought was a good idea and said I'd help if I could."

Another entry, dated June 5, 1958, said in part:

"Z evidently going full steam ahead on Quaker article. We had a good lunch and Z asked considerable detail about the great disruptions of 1827–28 when Elias Hicks rose up against the new Evangelism of that period and championed the older quietism. Interesting talk. I find Z an acute, intelligent person."

Zaostrovtsev and Harrison continued meeting, sometimes with others but usually alone (Zaostrovtsev was now telling Harrison he needed practice in English, and found the State Department officer a good teacher), and in time the Soviet diplomat said he finished the article.

He had sent it to a magazine in Russia and he told Harrison that there would be substantial payment. The article, Zaostrovtsev said, had come off particularly well and the magazine even asked him for another, this one on the background and training of junior foreign service officers. At the Russian's request, Harrison supplied him with some material available to the public on foreign service training.

For the next several weeks, Harrison saw little of the Russian. But in early September, Zaostrovtsev called excitedly to say that he had just received three hundred dollars from the Soviet publication for the Quaker article, "and I insist that you accept half of it."

Harrison refused and that seemed to end the matter. But at their next meeting, the Soviet diplomat again made the offer and this time placed fifteen new ten-dollar bills in Harrison's hands.

Again Harrison protested, but the Russian diplomat was adamant, saying (much as Kurochkin had insisted with Charles Beaumet):

"I could not have written the article without your help. This is a purely professional transaction; I would expect the same from you."

Harrison accepted the money and that night a portion of his diary read:

". . . hard to believe I'm involved in a Russian spy plot, but the FBI is convinced Z is softening me up for a coup. Actually hesitated about going to FBI, but realized I had been put in a compromising situation and knew I had to report it for my own protection, as well as my country's. The FBI contention that all Soviet diplomats double as intelligence agents is of course true, yet I find it both surprising and exciting to be involved personally. Must not tip my hand to Z . . ."

After a short period of silence, Zaostrovtsev invited Harrison for lunch and said that the Soviet magazine had liked the foreign service article and hoped that the Russian diplomat would be able to provide others on a continuing basis.

"Naturally I hope to do so," Zaostrovtsev said. "In my country, you know, writers are greatly admired. I think if I become a successful journalist, perhaps someday I'll be able to teach and write and live like a country gentleman. I hope from time to time I can call on you for help."

"I'll do what I can," said Harrison.

"Fine. Perhaps you could suggest an article now? Some general interest article about the American Government? There's a great curiosity about the workings of your government among my countrymen, just as there is among your countrymen about mine."

Harrison frowned and thought for several seconds. Then he said deliberately, "I'll never make a writer. I can't think of a thing. To tell you the truth, my mind's been so occupied with Africa lately that I haven't been able to think of anything else."

"Africa?" Zaostrovtsev asked. "Why Africa?"

"Well, I've been told that my next assignment will take me to Africa. It might be in another two weeks to a month. Of course I don't know which country yet, and so I've been studying up on all of them."

"An exciting continent," the Russian said. "I have been there and have some knowledge of it myself. Ah! That shall be my next article. If you can let me have the information on Africa's economic and political affairs that you've been reading about, I'll submit the idea tomorrow."

In his meetings with the FBI, Harrison had been warned that at some point Zaostrovtsev would depart from his harmless inquiries and make the move for which everything else had been nothing more than preparation. The FBI had no idea what information the Russian might be after. But they told Harrison it would undoubtedly be classified and that Zaostrovtsev, a very polished, professional agent, would undoubtedly disguise his intentions subtly and unobtrusively.

As Harrison saw it, this was now that point, and he refused.

"But why can't you help me?" the Soviet diplomat asked. His surprise seemed feigned.

"Well," said the American, "the communications that I've been reading on Africa are pretty high level stuff. A lot of them are the analyses our own experts have spent months drawing up. All of it's confidential, and I'm afraid most of it is classified."

Zaostrovtsev flicked his hand in a gesture that in effect dismissed Harrison's statement as unimportant. "Classified!" he snorted. "We are professional government people," he said huffily. "We know how much absolute nonsense and unimportant trivia is labeled classified. My government has not yet de-classified, if you can believe it, the specifications of a World War I tank that not only has not been produced for forty years, but was a dismal failure besides. So let us not share our governments' naiveté about what is 'classified' and what is not."

Zaostrovtsev sat back and pondered his cigarette for a moment. "I'll tell you what," he said slowly. "If giving me the information will get you in some sort of silly trouble with your bosses, simply make copies of them on your lunch hour when no one is around— and they'll never know."

If there had been any doubts in Harrison's mind about Zaostrovtsev's intentions they were now dispelled. The American again refused, but modified the refusal by saying he would think about it.

The Soviet diplomat seemed to be satisfied. He called for the check (he always did when they dined together) and the two parted.

The Russian went to the Soviet Embassy.

Harrison went directly to the FBI.

Not surprisingly, Harrison never again heard from his Russian friend. Based on the information that the State Department officer provided them, the FBI put together a full file on the Soviet diplomat's activities in Washington and turned it over to the Justice Department.

On May 15, 1959, the State Department very quietly informed the Soviet Embassy that its cultural attaché, who ranked as a Second Secretary, was persona non grata in the United States. And two days later, his usefulness, at least in this country, forever ended, Eugeni Alekseevich Zaostrovtsev, went back to the Soviet Union.

Thus, another wave had broken on the American shore, and had now retreated.

But one thing was certain. Another was on its way.

7

From Press Releases to Flying Lessons

And just three weeks later another wave did burst on our shores, depositing a Soviet diplomat, supposedly to fill the gap left by Nikolai Ivanovich Kurochkin in the "press matters" department.

Conceivably, Petr Ezhov's duties actually entailed such routine work when he arrived on June 6, 1959, and over the next six months. But all at once the slender, dark-haired forty-one-year-old native of Pinza Oblast came to the attention of the FBI as a spy.

It wasn't hard to pick up Ezhov's espionage activities once he plunged into them on December 27, 1959, on a northeast Washington street corner. The FBI had been watching another Russian named Vladimir Glinsky, a Third Secretary, who had been contacting a commercial photographer. The latter, in turn, was apparently in touch with a "Navy friend" who was providing classified Navy photos for the Russians.

Actually the "Navy friend" was nonexistent and the classified

Navy photos and other material being turned over to Vladimir Glinsky by the photographer, whom we'll call Thomas Kerr, had all been provided by the FBI after screening by proper Government officials.

"This is Peter," said Glinsky as he introduced Ezhov to Kerr. "He is going to be your new contact in the future. I have been ordered home. You will find Peter just as generous as I have been with the money, but you will also have to keep on producing."

Ezhov wasted little time telling the photographer what he'd have to produce. They'd been sitting in Kerr's car, but the new Soviet agent felt uncomfortable.

"Let us take a walk," he suggested, opening the door. The three men strolled slowly along a residential block of M Street, their collars turned up against stiff winter gusts threatening to deliver the capital's first snowstorm of the year.

"I must ask you for something different this time," Ezhov said in a tone that sounded totally important. "I would like to obtain a Navy film catalog and also I wish you to find out the price of a motion picture copying machine. Do you think you can do this?"

Kerr shrugged. "I shouldn't have any trouble finding out about the copying machine," he said, stopping to think a second. "But about that film catalog . . . I'm not certain. But I'll certainly try."

He had answered precisely as the FBI would have wanted. But this was to be expected since he'd been under the G-men's guiding hand nearly eight months, ever since Vladimir Glinsky had come to Kerr's photography studio in Washington for a set of passport photos. Out of this simple visit had come requests for aerial photos of Washington which Kerr couldn't supply himself.

But his suspicions were aroused sufficiently to put him on the phone to the FBI. After that, he was playing both sides in a game that ultimately led the Soviets to make a demand on Kerr that was unprecedented in the annals of Soviet espionage in this country—

Glinsky had directed Thomas Kerr to take flying lessons to qualify for a pilot's license so that he could take aerial photos of defense and military installations.

"And by the way," Ezhov asked casually as he and Glinsky walked Kerr back to his car, "how are you doing with your lessons?"

"Not so good," the photographer complained. "I'm a little low on cash and I haven't been able to enroll in the school."

"Nonsense," snapped Petr. "You make arrangements right away to take instructions and I will reimburse you."

The Russian pulled out a large wallet and withdrew five crisp ten-dollar bills. "Here," he commanded, "this should be more than enough for the first lesson."

Kerr took the money. "Okay, I'll get started right away."

Then Vladimir Glinsky offered his hand. "Good-bye, my friend," he smiled. "It has been very nice working with you. I will think of you often when I am back home. Perhaps someday we shall meet again."

Thomas Kerr saw no more of Glinsky who, as the FBI soon learned, actually had been recalled by Moscow and left the country on January 3, 1960.

The next rendezvous with Petr Ezhov, or Peter as Glinsky knew him, was scheduled for a residential block on Monroe Street in northeast Washington for six P.M. January 17. At that time, Kerr was to deliver the catalog he had promised to obtain from his "Navy friend." If, however, he could get it sooner, he was to give Ezhov a signal by double-parking in front of the French Embassy at one P.M. on January 15. This would tell the Soviet agent the material was ready and the two would meet at eight o'clock that night at the Monroe Street location.

The earlier delivery date was decided by the FBI. They wanted to spot Kerr's new Soviet contact—and get a daylight picture of him with their hidden cameras. Shutters clicked as a sedan bearing diplomatic plates issued to the Soviet Union cruised down the street past Kerr's double-parked car. When the films were developed an hour later and checked at the photo gallery of Soviet Embassy diplomats, the FBI identified their man:

Petr Ezhov
Birth data—Born 9-10-21, Pinza Oblast, USSR
Height—5'10"
Weight—160 pounds
Build—Medium
Hair—Dark Brown
Eyes—Gray
Complexion—Medium

His rank was listed as Third Secretary, replacing the now-departed Vladimir Glinsky. What his record didn't show was his new assignment—espionage.

By four P.M. Thomas Kerr had been shown Petr Ezhov's photo and he'd identified it as "Peter," his new Soviet contact.

By eight P.M. Kerr was at the designated location on Monroe Street—but there was no Ezhov.

The FBI instructed the photographer to keep his regular appointment with Ezhov on the night of the 17th. At six P.M., Kerr pulled up in his car, sat behind the wheel waiting, and in a few minutes he spotted "Peter" walking toward him.

"Good evening, Tom," said Ezhov, opening the door and getting into the front seat. "I am sorry we could not get together the other night. What happened to you?"

Kerr was puzzled. "I was here, but you weren't."

Ezhov laughed. "I see we did not understand each other. I was under the impression we were to meet on M Street, the same place as the last time. I went there and waited. When you did not show up, I became very worried. But I am glad it was only a misunderstanding. I shall try to make instructions clearer from now on."

Then Ezhov looked at Kerr with some anxiety.

"Did you get the manual?" His eyes shifted to a large brown paper-wrapped package on the floor under the dashboard.

"Is that it?"

Kerr nodded. "I wasn't able to get the Navy film catalog. I'm still working on that. But I got the training manuals that Vladimir asked for." He kicked the package lightly with the point of his shoe. "There they are—twenty-five books on Navy training procedures. Really good stuff."

Ezhov seemed disappointed. "That is good, but it is the Navy film catalog that I must have now. How soon will you be able to get it?"

"I'm not sure," replied Kerr. "You see, I don't want to arouse my Navy friend's suspicions. If I ask too much from him, he's liable to start wondering what's going on. Do you understand?"

"Yes, yes," snapped Ezhov. "By all means I agree with you. It must be done discreetly and with caution."

After some thought, Ezhov suggested that it might not be a bad idea if Kerr developed "social relationships" with other Navy men who might obtain material for him in the future.

"That's smart," Kerr said. "I'll go to work on them."

"And by the way," said the Soviet agent, "you must be on the lookout for Navy training films. I would like very much to get some of those. Do you think you can find them? It will be just a matter of borrowing them for one night. You know, just long enough so I can make copies. That is why I asked you to get me the price of the motion picture copying machine. Did you get it?"

Kerr reached into his pocket for a small brochure of the Bell and Howell Company. "It's all in here, Peter. They've got the prices listed on several models."

Ezhov took the brochure, then reached down for the package of Navy manuals. "Well, I will say thank you and wish you good night. Let us meet again on the thirty-first." He designated 7th and Quackenbos streets, and set eight P.M. as the time.

After getting out of the car, Ezhov suddenly remembered something and came back.

"You didn't tell me, how are you coming along with your flying lessons?"

Kerr replied that he had enrolled at a Washington flying school and was attending class twice weekly. "Good, good," the Russian said and walked to his car.

When they met on January 31, Kerr found Ezhov somewhat annoyed over the last delivery of Navy training manuals.

"They are nothing but junk," he complained. "Anyone can get them in any bookstore. I don't need any more manuals. What I want is the film catalog. Did you get that?"

The photographer said his "Navy friend" had promised to have a catalog, but wasn't able to put his hands on one yet.

"He'll get it," Kerr assured Ezhov. "Just be patient. It could be just a matter of days."

The Soviet diplomat emphasized how important the catalog was.

"I cannot ask you to get me the films unless I know what films there are. I also must know if you can procure the films on a regular basis to make it worthwhile for us to buy the motion picture copying machine. So everything is being held up. That is not too good."

"You've just got to have patience, Peter," the photographer said. "I'm doing my best."

"All right," returned the Russian. "I am not pushing you, my friend. But I want to make sure you understand how important it is that we get the catalog. Everything else depends on that."

Ezhov suddenly set forth still another demand, by far the boldest yet.

"I wonder how much trouble you will have getting your friend, or any other contact you develop in the Navy, to get classified material?" he asked bluntly.

"Classified material?" Kerr stammered.

"I know some of the manuals you had given Vladimir were classified, but many were not," the Russian said. "What I am referring to now are documents relating to naval operations which you could photograph yourself. I could furnish you a 'still copy outfit' to attach to your camera for photographing the documents. Your friend could take them out and you could photograph them."

"I just don't know," Kerr answered. "All I can tell you is that I'll try. I can't say any more than that right now."

The Russian accepted the answer. Then he questioned the photographer anew about his progress with the flying lessons. Kerr said he was getting along, but another payment was due at the school.

"How much?"

"Eighty dollars."

The Soviet Third Secretary counted out eight ten-dollar bills into Kerr's hand, then plunked two more tens into the pile. "That's a bonus," said Ezhov. Afterward he arranged another meeting with Kerr, for eight P.M., February 14, at Whittier and 6th streets.

Following the script prepared by the FBI, Kerr brought "good news" for Ezhov at their next get-together.

"My friend expects to give me the manual the day after tomorrow. I thought that would make you happy."

The word to Ezhov was nectar. He handed Kerr money to cover another bill for flying lessons, then introduced yet another and different element into the conspiracy.

"I would like you to take a few days off from work. Can you do it?"

"Why?" Kerr wanted to know.

Ezhov proceeded to explain—he wanted Kerr to make a visit to Norfolk, Virginia, but the specific instructions on what he was to do would come later.

"I can only take weekends off," Kerr said. "Would that be all right?"

"Very good," the Russian nodded. Then he told Kerr to meet him at the same place three nights from then, February 17.

"You will have the film catalog then, will you not?"

"That's a promise," Kerr answered.

The photographer proved a man of his word. He brought the alphabetical section of the Navy film catalog to the next meeting in a package covered with Christmas wrapping.

"There it is," he smiled, "that's from Santa Claus." Ezhov took it eagerly.

"Remember, Peter," Kerr said, "I've got to return it quickly. Before the end of the week."

"I shall have it back the night after tomorrow," the Soviet diplomat said. Then he looked at Kerr with another of his curious glances which invariably telegraphed some new demand.

"By the way," Ezhov began, "do you have any of the aeronautical charts you have been using in your flying lessons?"

"Yes, I have a few," Kerr replied. The FBI had wisely alerted him to expect such a request and had instructed him on how to answer. Such charts are always supplied to pilot trainees who must familiarize themselves with topography and landmarks of areas over which they take lessons.

"I'll bring them along the next time we meet," Kerr promised. Ezhov made a date for two nights from then, February 19, at the same time. But he changed the location back to one of their previous rendezvous, on M Street.

When the two got together again, Kerr gave Ezhov the aeronautical charts and Ezhov returned the Navy film catalog to Kerr. There was a dour look on Ezhov's face.

"It's no good," the Russian complained.

"What do you mean?" asked the photographer.

"It's an old one and the films listed there are only good for Navy enlistees," Ezhov pointed out.

But in the next breath he turned to Kerr and, pulling a piece of paper from his pocket, said, "See if you can get these for me."

Ezhov had written down four titles of "no good" films that he wanted Kerr to get anyway. "I want to see what they are about," the Russian said with a tone registering resignation. "I just wish you had that other film catalog—the big one with the classified films . . ."

The photographer told Ezhov he didn't think it was possible to get that one, but promised he'd try. Then the Russian questioned Kerr about the classified data. Kerr hedged, saying he was being tactful with his "Navy friend." "He might get suspicious if I rush him," he warned Ezhov.

The two met again on February 26, once more on M Street. Kerr had four 400-foot reels of 16mm. film that Ezhov had asked for. "I've got to get them back quickly," Kerr said. "My friend doesn't want to get in trouble."

"Tomorrow night," Ezhov promised.

The next night, at the same place, and same time, Ezhov returned the film. He didn't seem pleased. "All they show is how people should take care of themselves in case of fallout in an atomic attack. I have already seen these on American television."

Ezhov then told Kerr to try and get "confidential" Navy films. "I will pay more money for them," he promised. Kerr assured Ezhov he'd do what he could. Then once more the Russian inquired about the flying lessons and how soon Kerr might get his pilot's license.

"Oh, that'll be at least a few more months," Kerr said. "You know that learning to fly a plane isn't like driving a car."

"I know that," the Soviet diplomat returned. "The reason I am asking is that we are considering buying you a small plane for the aerial photography work we want you to do for us. How do you react to that?"

"Buy me a plane!"

"Yes, of course. We have lots of money and we want to spend it on you as long as you can deliver."

At the next meeting on March 13, Ezhov was ready with the details of Kerr's assignment in Norfolk. "I want you to go there

IN THE HIGHEST PLACES

First spy links between Soviet Embassy in Washington and Americans were bared in late 1940s and shock for nation was total when it learned accused included White House aide Alger Hiss (bottom photo), seated to the right of President Franklin D. Roosevelt and Secretary of State Edward R. Stettinius, Jr. at Yalta Conference. Josef Stalin and Winston Churchill are also at table. Fifteen months later, President Harry S Truman, with Stettinius and Major General Harry Vaughan (above left), greets Hiss at U.N. Conference in San Francisco. In photo right, Major General Claire L. Chennault, of "Flying Tigers" fame, shakes hands with Whittaker Chambers as another admitted Red agent, Elizabeth Bentley, looks on.

ALL PHOTOGRAPHS FROM UNITED PRESS INTERNATIONAL

FROM THE AGE OF INNOCENCE

Alger Hiss (left) now touches hands with common crook as he is led out of Federal Courthouse in New York City after being sentenced to five years for perjury because he lied about holding membership in Communist Party. His accuser was cherubic former *Time* Magazine editor Whittaker Chambers (below left), who claimed Hiss and others supplied him with Government secrets for transmission to Soviets. Revelations ended Age of Innocence for Americans who never believed such treachery could happen in their country.

TO THE AGE OF SUSPICION

Country was quickly stampeded into arms of flag-wavers, who believed anyone who ever rubbed elbows with a Russian had to be Red. Another victim of public wrath was Government economist William Remington (above), who also got three years for perjury because he denied membership in Communist Party. His accuser was matronly looking Elizabeth Bentley (left) who testified that Remington was one of her informers during World War II when she served as courier for Kremlin between Washington and New York "drop."

VICTOR PERLO

MAURICE HALPERIN

HAROLD GLASSER

TO THE AGE OF CONFUSION

The Age of Suspicion rapidly gravitated into the Age of Confusion when highly respected Americans such as the six (above) were cited at Senate Internal Security Subcommittee hearing as examples of Government officials who were promoted during Truman Administration despite "derogatory security information" turned up by investigators probing Communist infiltration and activity in nation's capital. What was worse for public than being told Hiss was a spy were allegations that White House was informed by FBI about security risks—and nothing was done.

KOVALEV

KUROCHKIN

MARTYNOV

PIVNEV

KIRILYUK

KRYLOV

AMOSOV

PETROV

FRANK COE

IRVING KAPLAN

ALGER HISS

THE REAL RED SPIES

GLADKOV

MOLEV

Here is partial gallery of Soviet officials serving in this country in diplomatic functions who were exposed by State Department while trying to steal or buy classified information. Diplomatic immunity spared these and all other Russians caught here as spies from jail. They were merely declared *persona non grata* and sent back to Moscow.

BUBOHIKOV

ABEL

HOW THE FBI GETS ITS SPY

When Russians sent Vladimir I. Gridnev to Washington to get in touch with brother, who had defected to U.S. years before, FBI trained long-range cameras on meeting, effected with help of Gennadiy G. Sevastyanov, attaché at Soviet Embassy. Series of photos (from left, above) shows Sevastyanov, in dark trenchcoat, and Gridnev waiting to rendezvous with defector at Virginia bus stop. Second panel shows Gridnev's brother arriving. FBI blocked out face to protect his identity. In third photo, Sevastyanov heads for car so Gridnev can give his brother "the pitch." Cupped hand technique is then employed for proposition: "You work for the United States Government . . . and there is information in your department that is very important in national security. Of course, the Soviet Union is most anxious to learn certain details about it, and we thought . . ." Gridnev's brother worked in the Pentagon—and he exposed the plot. Closeups at left show Sevastyanov (above) and Gridnev (below). At right is typical *persona non grata* departure scene. Yuri V. Novikov with wife, Klavdiya, and six-months-old daughter, Trina, are at New York City's La Guardia Airport after Washington demanded his recall as Second Secretary of Soviet Embassy because he had directed espionage plot.

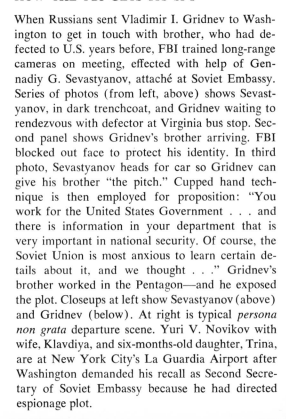

IN FROM THE HEAT

Airman Robert Glenn Thompson began feeding secrets to Reds at Rhein Main Air Force Base in Germany and continued after he returned to civilian life in U.S. When FBI caught up with him, he told all. He's shown at left being led out of FBI headquarters in New York after arrest. At right is Fedor Kudashkin, one of Thompson's contacts at Soviet Embassy. Below is Thompson's house on Long Island and one of trucks he used in fuel oil business. He got 30 years.

this weekend and take pictures of all the naval facilities," the Russian instructed with the casualness of a man asking his wife to take photos of the children.

"All the naval facilities?" Kerr gasped. "Do you have any idea how big a job that is? It would take a month, and even then no one can get to all the installations. They're very closely guarded."

Ezhov said he was aware of the enormity of the assignment. "Just do the best you can." He pressed Kerr's arm. "And also while you are there pick up any maps or booklets that have to do with military installations down there."

Kerr went to Norfolk and returned to meet Ezhov on March 25 outside the Madison Hotel at 15th and M streets. He handed the Russian a large bundle of photos, maps, and booklets (all hand-picked by the FBI). "Everything's there except for close-ups of the military and naval installations," Kerr apologized. "They're just too well guarded and I was afraid of arousing suspicion by getting too close. But you'll find some pretty good material here."

Ezhov slipped an envelope into Kerr's hand. "There's two hundred dollars for your trouble," winked the Soviet spy. "And I want to tell you that you can make a lot more money in the future if you can get more data."

"Swell," Kerr replied. "What's next?"

"Can you take time off in April? I want you to attend a convention in Los Angeles."

"What kind of a convention?"

"On air and space," the Russian whispered close to Kerr's ear. "But I will tell you more about it the next time."

They met again on the night of April 3 outside the Hay-Adams Hotel on 16th Street at H. When Kerr spotted the Russian coming toward him, he detected an unsteadiness in his walk.

"Good evening, Comrade," Ezhov drawled. Kerr knew immediately why Ezhov had trouble negotiating the sidewalk. He'd been drinking. But he still had his head about him.

"Your instructions are to go to the air and space exposition in Los Angeles on the twenty-first and look particularly at the type of aircraft on display and their fuel tank capacities."

The photographer wanted to know where the exposition was being held. "I have no idea, just someplace in Los Angeles," Ezhov said, oblivious to the geographic sprawl of California's largest and fastest growing city.

He patted Kerr on the shoulder. "You are a smart young man. You will find it when you get there, I am sure."

Kerr went to Los Angeles. But there was no exposition. The air and space event had been canceled.

To convince Ezhov that he wasn't lying, Kerr took a picture of the "closed" sign on the arena door. Then, to show good faith (an FBI suggestion), Kerr went to a symposium on manned space stations, and to another convention dealing with metals and minerals in the space age. He obtained armfuls of pamphlets, brochures, and handouts—all available to the public—and brought them for Ezhov at their next rendezvous on April 26 outside the Hay-Adams.

The Soviet agent was delighted with Kerr's enterprise. "I am happy to see you are using good judgment. The trip was not wasted. This calls for a bonus next time I see you."

Before Ezhov left he gave Kerr two more assignments—to attend an electronics exhibition and another on helicopters, both in Washington during May.

Kerr met Ezhov next at ten P.M. on July 4 at 5th Street and Florida Avenue. Kerr had arrived first, parked on Florida Avenue near the corner, and waited for Ezhov. The Russian arrived about ten minutes later, got into the photographer's car, and had him drive to 9th Street where Ezhov asked Kerr to park by the curb.

"Do you have the material?" asked the Russian.

Kerr got out, opened the trunk, and took out two shopping bags and a small suitcase crammed with pamphlets, brochures, handouts, and photographs of electronic devices and gadgets, as well as helicopters.

Ezhov took the material, walked to the corner, and handed it all to a man who had been waiting there. Kerr noticed the man was tall and slender and that he was dressed in a dark suit, but otherwise he was undistinguishable in the shadows where he'd been standing. He took the shopping bags and suitcase, crossed the street, got into an old model car, and barreled away at high speed.

Ezhov came back, reentered Kerr's car, and directed him to take a leisurely drive into the Maryland suburbs. The Russian wanted to talk. Kerr did, too. He wanted to know who the stranger was, but Ezhov brushed off the query with a curt, "He's a friend."

Then the Soviet agent brought up the flying lessons once more and wanted to know how far Kerr was from his pilot's license.

"Perhaps a month or so," he replied vaguely. "It's one of those things that I can't tell until my instructor says I'm ready. I'll know better when I ask him next time I take my lesson."

Kerr then reminded Ezhov that he hadn't been reimbursed for his trip to Los Angeles and for some of the other favors he'd done. The Russian thrust his hand into his pocket for his wallet with a sudden guilty impulse.

"Forgive me, my friend," he apologized. "Here, take this. Money means nothing."

He handed Kerr a thick wad of tens and when the photographer counted them later he was astounded to find they added up to an even five hundred dollars.

"Let's call it a going-away present," one of the FBI men kidded Kerr afterward. "Your work is finished—and so is Ezhov's."

The FBI had all the evidence it needed against the Third Secretary.

"What'll happen to him?" asked Kerr more out of curiosity than concern.

"Who knows?" The G-man smiled. "Perhaps he can handle

'press matters' in some other capital. He didn't pay much attention to his work while he was here."

On July 22, 1960, the State Department informed the Soviet Embassy that Petr Ezhov was persona non grata. Five days later, Ezhov, his wife, Irena, and their three-year-old daughter, Maria, boarded a trans-Atlantic jetliner at New York's International Airport on the first leg of their flight to Moscow.

The Soviet Embassy once again had a vacancy. And if it could have hung a "help wanted" sign on its door it might well have read:

"Opening for intelligent young man. Handle 'press matters' and double as spy. Experience necessary. Must be able to fool FBI. Also must know how to steer clear of Americans who make fools of Russian agents."

8

Big Brother Is Watching

Spring came early to Washington in 1963. The evening of April 28 had July-like temperatures that were a dread reminder of the long hot summer the capital endures each year. The city's celebrated Japanese cherry trees had bloomed days ago and their blossoms already littered the Potomac's banks like white confetti.

Yet this wonderful sight was one which the man we shall call Evgeni Gudrinski had few occasions to see. His work in the capital kept him so preoccupied he seldom took time to notice much of the Washington vista. He was like the man who lives a lifetime in New York and never visits the Statue of Liberty or the top of the Empire State Building.

Gudrinski was a handsome, straight cut of a man in his middle forties with rugged but warm features distinguished by combed-back black hair and thick brows that jutted like awnings over his dark, penetrating eyes. He was a "good and gentle, hard-working Russian," as authorities in Washington described him.

He was also a man of high principle and substance whose direction long ago had estranged him from the Marxist camp. Twenty-three years before, during the grim early days of World War II, he had fled his homeland and sought the freedom in the West he'd heard so much about. After the war, he spurned Soviet pressure to return home and was granted permission to stay in the United States.

Though he had courage and determination, Gudrinski dreaded the GPU and the reprisals it might spawn against him even here.

Gudrinski settled in Arlington and found employment at the Pentagon in a nonsensitive yet important Federal position. For fifteen years his work kept him occupied and happy. He was a man of ability and his labors were rewarded with frequent advances which ultimately placed him in charge of a section of some twenty employes. Everyone who worked with Gudrinski liked and respected him. He was serious and demanding in his job, yet he was also just and kind-hearted.

On this sultry April 28 evening the past must have seemed very distant to Evgeni Gudrinski as he ventured out into the rapidly gathering dusk on one of his infrequent strolls through Arlington's tree-lined streets.

The route this night took him to Arlington Ridge Road, which afforded a commanding view of the capital and the Virginia countryside. Below he could see the Pentagon, whose interior he knew well.

Gudrinski didn't linger long because it was getting dark. While he had shed many apprehensions about his safety, he was never fully convinced the Russians might not attempt someday to reach him and force his return to the "homeland." If they did, he had told himself, it would be furtively, most probably at an hour least likely to attract attention—at night.

Thus in darkness, the safest place, Gudrinski felt, was home in his modestly furnished apartment near Wilson Boulevard and Hudson Street. A bachelor, he had lived there alone since the development was built more than ten years before.

As Gudrinski approached his home intersection of Wilson and Hudson, night had fully descended. A look at his watch as he passed under the streetlight told him it was just nine o'clock.

Suddenly Gudrinski was startled by a voice calling his name.

"Evgeni! Evgeni!"

The inflection was distinctly Russian. Gudrinski felt a chill. He groped frantically through his mind to identify the voice. He didn't dare shorten his step or turn to see who it was as he wrestled with his memory.

"Evgeni!" the voice called again, this time more sharply. "What is the matter?" the words came in Russian. "Don't you want to talk to your own brother!"

Gudrinski halted abruptly. He wheeled around searching the darkness for the man who had just called to him. He caught sight of a shadowy figure twenty feet away at the curb beside a parked car.

As he peered steadily, the vague silhouette moved toward him, slowly at first, then with rapid steps. Finally the face was touched by the light filtering out from the apartment house foyer.

"Vladimir!" cried Gudrinski. Both men simultaneously threw their arms around each other.

The voice, the man, as though in a dream, really was the brother Gudrinski had left behind in Russia twenty-three years before.

Although they hadn't seen each other since, time had treated Vladimir kindly. He's hardly changed, Gudrinski thought, looking at the brother who was four years his senior.

"When did you arrive?" Gudrinski asked excitedly as they stepped into the brightly lighted foyer, studying each other's faces. "How did you ever find me? Why have you come to the United States?"

The long-missing brother cracked a wide smile at the torrent of questions.

"Just yesterday. But a minute, please, Evgeni," he taunted good-humoredly. "How can I answer so many questions? It will take more than a word or two to tell all that has happened and why I am here. . . . But this is not the place to talk."

Vladimir looked around with a frown. "Can't we go somewhere . . . where is your apartment?"

"Of course, Vladimir," he apologized. "My place is on the third floor. Come."

He led his brother by the arm to the elevator. The apartment was a modest bachelor's quarters, neatly furnished, spotlessly clean. It had a living room, bedroom, kitchen, and bath.

"This is truly a capitalist's home," joked the visitor in his casual inspection of the flat.

"Tell me, dear brother," Vladimir asked as he finally settled deep into a soft armchair in the living room. "Why have we not heard from you all these many years? You didn't come back to see us—you didn't even write. Why?"

Gudrinski remained silent for a long interval. Finally he turned to his brother, looked at him squarely, and spoke in a low, deliberate voice.

"You know I could not have visited. . . . And if I had written it would have been bad for the family. I did not want to have anyone hurt. You know what the police could have done."

Vladimir stared back somberly for a moment, then grinned almost sardonically. "You, dear brother, are so silly to think that you could not have come back to live in the motherland—"

Evgeni quickly interrupted. "I did not say I would have come back to live there. I am very happy here. This is my homeland now. This is a wonderful country, and I would not leave it for anything. What I am saying is that I could not have gone back even for a visit. You know very well the authorities would never let me leave. It would have meant Siberia . . . or even worse."

Vladimir shook his head. "You are so wrong. As one who is

about to become an American citizen you could not have been held there against your will. You should know that."

Evgeni looked at his brother contemplatively. How did he know about his plans for citizenship? How, indeed, he wondered had Vladimir been able to come to the United States and in a country of 190,000,000 people and a 3,000-mile stretch of continent find him? Through all the years, Evgeni had never written to anyone in Russia to reveal his whereabouts.

He gave Vladimir a questioning look. "How did you find me?" he demanded. "Who helped you?"

Vladimir shuffled uneasily in his chair. "I think you have become contaminated with that disease that is so common to the Americans—we call it distrust."

"But it is so very strange that you can arrive in the country one day, and find me the very next day when you had no idea where I might be," Vladimir returned bluntly. "I think you are not telling me everything—"

The doorbell interrupted him. "I wonder who that can be?" Evgeni frowned as he rose from the sofa and walked to the door.

Vladimir watched his brother, knowing full well whom Evgeni would find at the door.

"Evgeni Gudrinski, I presume," said the tall, broad-shouldered stranger standing in the hall as Gudrinski opened the door. "Allow me to introduce myself. I am Ivan Ivanovich, your brother's chauffeur."

Gudrinski turned and shot a questioning glance at his brother. Why the slyness, he thought? Why didn't Vladimir mention that his "chauffeur" would call? How did he know where to find Vladimir? And what position did his brother hold to command a chauffeur?

Evgeni didn't betray his annoyance which was quickly turning to suspicion.

"Come in, Mr. Ivanovich," he invited.

"Forgive me for not mentioning that Ivan was coming up,"

Vladimir apologized. "I forgot to tell you in the excitement of see-ing you after all these years, dear Evgeni. Ivan was good enough to accept the assignment to drive me around Washington."

"Assignment from whom?" Gudrinski demanded, trying to temper his voice. If this was an "assignment" it must have come from the only place such "assignments" are commissioned. The Russian Embassy! What were his brother and this stranger up to?

"Evgeni," began the new visitor, after being invited to sit down. "No doubt you are wondering how your brother was able to find you. The truth is that we have been searching for you for many months—"

"Who has been searching for me?" interrupted Gudrinski.

"The Soviet Embassy," said the man who called himself Ivan Ivanovich. "You see, your brother had appealed to officials in Mos-cow to help us find you. And we are always eager to cooperate with our citizens."

Evgeni listened intently. He was anxious to hear out this man from the Soviet Embassy. There had to be much more to the story of how they had found his haven.

"We found you some months ago," Ivanovich said. "We have kept a very close watch over your activities, over your movements. We were able to learn all about you, about your duties at the Pen-tagon. Believe me, the portrait we have of you is rather complete."

"Why? . . . Why?" interrupted Gudrinski, suddenly terrified. He hadn't been ignorant of the Soviets' ability to hunt down some-one they were determined to find. Yet, after all this time, after he had almost begun to believe those who told him not to worry, why should the Soviet Embassy suddenly take such interest in him? Cer-tainly not because his brother was looking for him, if there was any truth to that.

"You see, Comrade Evgeni," the man who claimed he was a chauffeur went on, almost as if reading Gudrinski's thoughts, "we have a very important task for you."

"What kind of task?" Gudrinski said belligerently. He was suddenly more angry than frightened.

"Please, Comrade," Ivanovich said curtly. "If you interrupt I shall not be able to tell you. I beg you to listen."

Gudrinski gazed stoically at the speaker.

"Your brother came here to make you a very fine proposition. It will be most rewarding to you. It will be a chance to prove your worthiness to the people you left so many years ago. But let Comrade Vladimir explain it."

"Well, my brother," Evgeni asked. "What is this proposition?"

"It is quite important, Evgeni . . ." Vladimir shuffled nervously in his chair. "You work for the United States Government . . . and there is information in your department that is very important to national security. Of course, the Soviet Union is most anxious to learn certain details about it, and we thought . . ."

Vladimir looked searchingly at his brother. Vladimir seemed reluctant to lay all his cards on the table. But the cards Evgeni had seen so far told him his brother had come with a pat hand.

"Here is what I am trying to say, brother Evgeni," Vladimir started again. "I have been delegated to make contact with you and to ask you to work for the Soviet Union. And I have been authorized to promise you that you can return to our homeland and expect to be well taken care of."

As he spoke, Vladimir tilted his head toward Ivanovich. He wanted him to bear out what he was saying.

"It is all true," the latter put in. "We would not have brought your brother all the way here merely to play a trick on you. In all honesty, we need your help—but we want to reward you for it."

Gudrinski asked Ivanovich what his official role was in the negotiation.

"Let us for now say I am just your brother's chauffeur," he replied evasively.

"And what is your position, Vladimir?" Gudrinski turned to his brother. "Are you with the KGB?"

"Of course not," Vladimir began to laugh. "You are thinking now the way of Americans. They believe everyone from Russia is a spy. My position is with the Scientific Institute for Cattle-Raising and Animal Husbandry. My office is in the bureau headquarters at Frunze."

"Then why are you trying to get me to spy on my adopted country?" Evgeni asked, his tone still edged with annoyance.

Vladimir got up from his chair and walked over to his brother. "My dear Evgeni. You don't owe this country anything. Your allegiance is to the Soviet Union. But more important, it is about your brothers and sisters that you must think. It is for them—and for me—that I ask you to consider this. And most of all for yourself. What future do you have here? If you come back to Russia, you will have an important job and all the riches you ever dreamed about . . ." Vladimir studied his brother in silence for several long moments, waiting for him to respond.

Evgeni finally asked brusquely, "What is it you want from me?"

"Not in anger," returned Vladimir, putting his hand lightly on Evgeni's shoulder. "You should be happy and proud—"

Evgeni's sudden turnabout and apparent resignation to Vladimir's offer evoked little surprise from the man who made the proposition, or from his companion. It seemed they had taken it for granted the defector would come around.

A sheepish grin broke over Evgeni's face now and his visitors began relaxing in an atmosphere where tension all at once seemed to have vanished.

"You know," Evgeni began slowly, "I cannot guarantee you anything . . . I may have nothing to offer that you do not already know. My work is not that secret—"

"Please," interrupted Ivanovich, "that is not for you to say. Let us decide what is important. Agreed?"

Evgeni shrugged resignedly.

Their pact was sealed, delivered!

The rest of the evening passed in an atmosphere of conviviality and merriment with not another word about the espionage role just consigned to Evgeni Gudrinski. With the charm and graciousness of a perfect host, he brought out a bottle of vodka and poured his guests drinks. He toasted to their health—and even to "my motherland, the Union of Soviet Socialist Republics."

Before leaving, Evgeni's visitors made a final mention of the agreement. They wanted to see him again two days later, April 30. The rendezvous was arranged by Ivanovich, who told Evgeni that he and Vladimir would meet him at a bus stop near Wilson Boulevard and Hudson Street in Arlington at seven o'clock in the evening.

On the appointed day, at the exact hour they had agreed, Evgeni met the two men. They were waiting at the corner when he arrived on foot and they greeted him warmly.

"Come, Comrade," Ivanovich urged Evgeni, "we will go somewhere that we can talk."

Evgeni appeared fretful. His brother detected it. "What is wrong, Evgeni?" he asked.

"Nothing. I had a very hard day at work and I am tired. Do not worry about me. I am all right."

They took him to a black 1963 Pontiac sedan parked at the curb on Hudson Street, some fifty feet from the bus stop. Ivanovich opened the back door and urged the two brothers to sit in the rear. Then he walked around and, playing the chauffeur's role faithfully, slid in behind the wheel.

As they drove off, Evgeni asked Ivanovich if he was really a chauffeur.

"I am sure you must work for the Soviet Embassy in Washington," Evgeni said probingly, "but I don't think that you are just a man to drive other people around—"

"What do you think I am, then?" Ivanovich interrupted.

"Oh, I thought perhaps you might be one of the consuls or someone higher than a mere chauffeur."

"Your brother is very analytical," Ivanovich quipped to Vladimir. "I think he is going to work out very well."

The drive was brief. Ivanovich pulled into a parking lot on Wilson Boulevard and turned off the motor. "Come," he commanded, "let us go in here." It was a restaurant.

They took a table against the wall midway down the right side of the dining room. As the waiter brought menus, Ivanovich suddenly stood up. "I am sorry but I just remembered I have an errand to perform," he apologized. "But I will be back shortly." He excused himself and left the restaurant.

The brothers decided to have cocktails and await Ivanovich's return before ordering dinner. After the waiter brought the drinks, Vladimir and Evgeni chatted as casually as if discussing the comparative breeding of Soviet and American cattle herds. Or so it would have seemed to the casual observer. But in fact Vladimir was giving his brother "final instructions" on what he was to do in the plot to spy against his adopted country.

"In a few days," Vladimir said, "I must return home. I hope you will get along with Ivan. He will be your contact. You will supply him with the information he requests. And please keep in mind at all times your relatives at home. Don't do anything to endanger us. In the end, when you return to us, you will find the happiness that has escaped you all these years of your lonely existence."

Evgeni mulled over the implied threat of reprisals against his family. Then almost hesitantly he asked his brother, "What can they do if, shall we say, I don't live up to the bargain?"

Vladimir grimaced.

"You know better than to ask, dear brother. I need not tell you what it is to be damned."

The brothers' conversation was interrupted by Ivan, who had returned, visibly excited.

"I don't think we should eat here," he said ominously. "There is not enough privacy."

Ivanovich called for the check, paid it, and walked the brothers out to the car. Evgeni noted that the Pontiac was in the same parking space in the lot as it was when they drove to the restaurant. Wherever Ivanovich had gone on his mysterious trip, he must have walked—or ridden in another car.

They reentered the car and drove in search of another restaurant. After a while they were in Falls Church, a neighboring community of Arlington, but they couldn't find a restaurant that Ivanovich thought was suitable. They continued west on Route 7 to a small shopping center outside the town and there Ivan spotted a grill that he said would be a good place to eat. They parked and went in.

It was eight-thirty P.M. and the restaurant had very few late diners.

"This is much better," Ivanovich said as he scanned the empty tables. "Here we can talk."

They sat toward the back of the restaurant. Speaking in a low voice, Ivanovich began detailing what the Russians hoped was to be a master espionage plan in the Pentagon, to be executed by Evgeni Gudrinski. He was to steal information the Soviets sought and deliver it into their hands.

"When we ask you for something, you will tell us if it is within your reach. If it is not, we will want to know who is the person who can supply that information. We will want his name and address, his position at the office, and anything you know about his background, his financial status, his friends and associates . . ."

The instructions were lengthy. Ivanovich didn't miss a detail. And Evgeni Gudrinski listened intently, somewhat bewildered by the flood of demands. The threat of reprisals against members of his family in the event Evgeni didn't go with the ploy, which his brother had alluded to, was repeated now, forcefully, by Ivanovich.

"It would not put your brother in a good position, nor his family, if you let them down on this assignment. You don't want anything to happen to them, I am sure."

"No! No!" Evgeni cried. "I don't want them hurt. I will do nothing to harm them."

Ivanovich next spelled out a plan of meetings between Evgeni and himself. They were to be held in public, yet they entailed considerable secrecy and care.

"What of my brother?" asked the Government employee with puzzlement. "Is he going to meet with us too?"

"Vladimir is leaving very shortly," Ivanovich replied quickly. "He must go home. The Americans allowed him only a thirty-day visa and it is almost over. But you will not be separated from him. You will write each other. I will serve as your courier. You will give me your letters to Vladimir and I will deliver his to you."

"Then I shall not see you anymore?" Evgeni turned to Vladimir. "You mean . . . this is good-bye?"

"No," the brother answered. "We shall see each other again. Day after tomorrow. I will be leaving by the end of the week, perhaps Saturday."

They agreed to meet in front of Arlington's Glebe Theater, on North Glebe Road at seven thirty P.M. "Vladimir and I shall come by in the car and pick you up," Ivanovich said.

Finally the three men ordered dinner. During the meal Ivanovich plied Evgeni with questions about the work he was doing for the Government, about others employed in his department, and the routines of the office. Evgeni spoke openly about his own work, which he insisted wasn't vital, but was guarded with his answers to the other queries. "I just don't know too much about them," he'd say. "But now that I know you are interested, I will be trying to find out more."

Ivanovich paid the check after they finished. Evgeni was driven to a corner about three blocks from his apartment and let out.

"It is best we drop you off here," Ivanovich said. "We do not want anyone who may know you to see us together. Remember we must exercise great care at all times."

The following Thursday, May 2, Evgeni left his job at the Pentagon at the end of his work day at five P.M. and headed for what was to be the last meeting with his brother. On the way, he had stopped at his apartment to pick up several gift packages for his relatives in Russia.

Promptly at seven thirty a late-model green Chevrolet pulled up to the curb where Evgeni was standing and the man on the passenger's side stuck his head out the front window.

"My brother, I see you have been shopping," he smiled.

It was Vladimir. Beside him sat the driver, Ivanovich, grinning broadly.

"You have changed cars, I see," Evgeni said curiously.

"Get in, brother," Vladimir said after helping Evgeni load the packages into the back while listening to what he had bought for the relatives back home. "There is a little gift for you, too, Vladimir," said Evgeni, handing him a small red-wrapped box containing one of the new gas-type cigarette lighters.

Evgeni sat in front with the other two men as they cruised slowly along Wilson Boulevard. During the drive Ivanovich did most of the talking. He went over ground he'd already covered, striving to make it clear to Evgeni how important it was to be punctual when they scheduled meetings.

After driving a distance along Wilson Boulevard, they had maneuvered through some side streets and started back on Wilson. As they went past the Glebe Theater again, Ivanovich said to Evgeni, "Take a look at the cinema here, do you see it? This is where we shall meet at nine o'clock at night on the second Thursday of each month, starting in June. You will go there and wait for me near the box office until I come by."

Then he proceeded to brief the Government employee on his first assignment in espionage.

"I want a list of the people who work in your department . . . their names, the jobs they do, and where they live. Bring the list with you when we meet."

Ivanovich brought the car to a stop at the bus stop near Gudrinski's home. "We had better say good-bye now," the driver told Evgeni. "Vladimir must prepare for his departure tomorrow."

The two brothers shook hands and embraced on the sidewalk. They promised to write each other and parted after Vladimir half-whispered in Evgeni's ear, "Don't let the family down, brother. We are depending on you."

Six weeks later, the night of June 18, 1963, Evgeni Gudrinski arrived at the Glebe Theater at eight fifty-eight P.M., two minutes early for his first meeting with the man who'd been calling himself Ivan Ivanovich. Promptly at nine P.M. he caught sight of the hulking figure of the Soviet agent at the end of the block walking toward him.

Gudrinski, who was holding a small manila envelope in his hand, waved it vigorously toward the approaching man in an apparent attempt to attract his attention.

Ivanovich saw Evgeni flourishing the envelope and lifted his hand in recognition.

At this very moment, however, the raised envelope and the wave from Ivanovich also drew attention from six FBI agents!

The G-men were staked out in three locations, two at a window on the second floor of a building across the street, one in a doorway near the theater, and three in a car parked at the curb near the theater. They were there to continue the rigid surveillance they had begun on Evgeni Gudrinski on the evening of April 30 when they recorded his first outside meeting with his brother and Ivanovich, at the bus stop in Arlington, and had followed them to that first restaurant.

The G-men had even shadowed the three men to the grill outside Church Falls where they had dinner and talked over the plot to pilfer information from the Pentagon. More than ever then, the FBI agents knew they had to keep an eye on things, for when Ivanovich left briefly from the restaurant on Wilson Boulevard, he was seen getting into a car driven by another man.

He was taken to the Soviet Embassy in Washington—then back to the restaurant.

On May 2, when they had met again for Evgeni's and Vladimir's good-byes and the presentation of going-away gifts, all three men were in the FBI's sights from start to finish of their drive back and forth on Wilson Boulevard.

Not only was every move watched—it was documented on motion picture as well as still camera film.

After the initial batch of film was developed, the FBI knew with whom it was dealing, for Ivanovich was recognized at once. It was not the first time the Bureau had spotted him in a clandestine scheme.

Once before, in the late fall of 1959, he had come under scrutiny in an ill-fated plot to get information about the CIA and Army Intelligence.

The FBI had then learned his real name—Gennadiy Sevastyanov—and quite a bit about his pedigree. He was born in Russia on February 7, 1930, and had arrived in the United States on March 31, 1959, to serve as an attaché in the cultural division of the Soviet Embassy.

Vladimir's true name has been withheld by the FBI. If it were known, his brother whom we've identified as Evgeni Gudrinski would also lose the anonymity he desires—and richly deserves.

He deserves that status because he demonstrated unusual gratitude and loyalty to his adopted country. For the very morning following his brother's and Sevastyanov's visit to his apartment, Evgeni Gudrinski went to his office in the Pentagon, sought out his superior, and informed him of what had happened.

The FBI was notified. Agents went to the Pentagon and interviewed Evgeni, who told them everything that had been said the night before.

"Gentlemen," he said to the agents in a voice on the verge of tears, "I don't know what to do. After all these years, they bring my brother over here to persuade me into espionage against the country I love. I am a man who wants to be a United States citizen. I understand the true difference between Soviet enslavement and American freedom."

Then with anger rising in his voice, Evgeni continued:

"The implied threat of reprisals against members of my family and the assurance of good pay and a good job for me later in the Soviet Union—all these have fallen on ears that are sensitive to the lies and deceit employed by Soviet intelligence agents. I will not betray the United States. But you must tell me what to do. I need your help and guidance."

The FBI agents complimented Gudrinski for good sense in leading his brother and Sevastyanov into believing he'd go to bat for the Soviet Union. Now the G-men could have their inning against these Kremlin agents.

"Keep stringing them along," instructed one of the agents. "Meet them where they tell you, promise to deliver what they ask. Then report to us exactly what happened and what was said. We'll guide you—and we guarantee you all the protection you'll need."

From that moment on, Gudrinski's last meeting with Sevastyanov outside the Glebe Theater was evidence enough to pave a hurried path back to Moscow. The stills and movies, shot at night with infrared film, showed Evgeni handing "Ivan" the manila envelope —which, significantly, was the cue to the FBI men to start their cameras rolling and clicking. His wave of greeting to the approaching Soviet agent had been the signal to the G-men.

In the envelope which he handed to Sevastyanov were a list of names, addresses, and job duties at the Pentagon. The Russian agent accepted them with glee and instructed Gudrinski to give him a detailed report about the department's operations at their next meeting on the second Thursday of July.

Actually the data handed to the Soviet agent were carefully prepared by the FBI.

Even the gifts for the relatives that Evgeni gave Vladimir were purchased by the FBI. They were lures to lend weight to the defector's capitulation and sincerity in the plot.

There was no meeting between Evgeni Gudrinski and the man he knew as Ivan Ivanovich on that second Thursday, the 15th day of July, 1963. Not any meetings thereafter.

Gennadiy Sevastyanov, alias "Ivan Ivanovich," departed for the USSR before he could keep that appointment, hastened by the State Department which declared him persona non grata.

As for Evgeni Gudrinski, he is still employed in the Pentagon. Since this case, he has received another promotion and his future with the Government seems to hold promise of even further advancement.

He felt no regrets about letting down his brother—or his relatives in Russia. He sensed no obligation to them, for it took twenty-three long years for someone from his family to get in touch. None of the letters he had written to his old homeland after he had arrived here had ever been answered. It was only when the Kremlin espionage factory felt he might be of some use that his family responded.

Evgeni Gudrinski, who finally gave up efforts to reach his family, changed his name, and severed all ties with the past, felt he owed the relatives nothing—not even a sympathetic letter should his brother Vladimir's address have changed now from Tambov to Siberia.

9

The American Who Came from Berlin

"ROBERT GLENN THOMPSON RETURNING TO STATES . . . PROBABLE
FIRST STOP WITH WIFE AT 14 HENDRIE STREET DETROIT . . . DEPAR-
TURE 1-15-58 . . ."

This cabled message from the 7493rd Special Investigation Wing,
an intelligence branch of the Air Force's Office of Special Investigation at the Rhein Main Air Force Base in Frankfurt, Germany,
was flashed to the Pentagon January 7, 1958.

An hour later it was relayed to the FBI, and a tail was put on
twenty-three-year-old Airman Second Class Robert Glenn Thompson, stationed at the huge Tempelhof Air Base in West Berlin as a
clerk in the Military Special Investigations office. But a watch on
the hulking six-foot-two, 250-pounder had begun many months
before.

His visits to East Berlin, his drinking, his sudden supply of extra spending money, and a peculiar irregularity in his work had tended to attract attention, then suspicion, and finally, surveillance.

Although he was unaware of it, Thompson had been observed snapping pictures with a small camera of confidential and secret reports that crossed his desk. Thompson was allowed to continue in his sensitive position, although the Air Force now made certain that no reports of value were routed across his desk, because the OSI was trying to determine what other American airmen, if any, and what Russian agents might be involved with him. But when a reasonable period of time had passed with no such indications, the Air Force decided to send Thompson back to the United States, to Malmstrom Air Force Base, Montana. Authorities assumed that if Thompson was indeed as deeply involved in espionage as the OSI suspected, he would continue these activities at his new post.

Even as Thompson was crossing the Atlantic en route to a stop-over in Detroit to see his wife, the FBI was studying his dossier.

It was a complex of paradoxes. His service records bore out that he was in some ways a capable clerk of average intelligence with more ability than might be expected of the high school dropout he was. Thompson was born in Detroit on January 30, 1935, the first of two children of Robert and Bernice Thompson. His mother first took him and his sister to live with their grandparents; then, they made a home of their own.

In December, 1952, when only seventeen, Robert Glenn Thompson enlisted in the Air Force with his mother's consent. He finished in the top three in his class at aircraft and engine mechanics school at Shepard Air Force Base in Wichita Falls, Texas, and served briefly as a mechanic with a B-29 squadron until he fell off a platform and injured his back. That put him into a desk job and ultimately, in January, 1954, he was sent to Germany, where he was assigned to OSI.

Almost immediately Thompson began to drink heavily in his off-duty hours, carouse with women, and in general lead a raffish life.

But at work he was dependable and could be counted on to carry out his duties with surprising skill.

Then in the spring of 1955, he met Evelyn Matthes, eighteen, a tall German redhead whom he married the following February. They moved into an apartment on the Unter den Eichen in West Berlin and, briefly, Thompson eased up on his drinking.

A wife, and even the birth of a daughter, weren't enough influence; Thompson went out one night with another airman, got drunk, lost his .38 caliber revolver, stole one from the supply room to replace it, and was court-martialed.

Broken in rank from first class airman to second, Thompson brooded and began to act strangely. His trips across the border into East Berlin were noticed and he was followed.

During this surveillance by the OSI's intelligence section, Thompson's morale seemed to hit bottom. Part of the punishment after the court-martial was a withdrawal of certain privileges including living off the base which meant his wife and child had to be sent to the United States to make their home. They went to Detroit, where his mother lived, and settled in a small apartment at 14 Hendrie Street. Thompson was infuriated by the separation.

When he returned home on January 15, 1958, he went straight to his wife. The stopover in Detroit was no longer than a week, the time he was allowed in his travel orders, and FBI agents found his movements anything but suspicious.

They watched Thompson go shopping with his wife on busy Woodward Street; they saw him and his wife and child visit his mother in the city, and they observed him when he went to a used-car lot and bought a 1955 station wagon. The G-men also were nearby when Thompson loaded the family's belongings into the back of the wagon and, with his wife, baby, and a dog they had brought over from Germany, drove westward to Montana.

The shadow on the hulking airman was thorough—and relentless. He was followed across the country by a covey of FBI men. When Thompson and the family stopped at a motel in Great Falls, just outside Malmstrom Air Force Base, when he checked in at the base, and later went out and bought a house trailer for two hundred dollars down and sixty a month, the FBI was never far behind.

The G-men found nothing suspicious in what Robert Glenn Thompson had done in the first two weeks of his return to the States until one afternoon he entered an appliance store and bought a short-wave radio with a special antenna for two hundred and fifty dollars, then stopped in a photography shop to purchase a 35-mm. still camera which cost one hundred and fifty dollars. The reasons for Thompson's expensive tastes were not immediately forthcoming because, otherwise, he continued to act like any other serviceman-husband. He went to the base each day, performed his duties in the clerical pool—he was now in a nonsensitive position—at the Strategic Air Command post, and went home at night to be with his wife and child.

However, not long after he bought the radio and camera, Thompson went to the post office in Great Falls, and rented a mail box—No. 871.

Some weeks later, the FBI spotted Thompson and his wife driving away from the trailer. They followed the couple to a hospital where Mrs. Thompson remained. The G-men learned later that the airman's wife, who was pregnant again, had to be confined to the hospital because she was ill. Thompson went back to the trailer.

Now, for the first time, the FBI—which had bugged the trailer— heard the radio's short-wave band in action. For a day or two it picked up nothing significant. But then, late one evening, the G-men heard a voice with a patently Russian intonation saying what sounded like *"Amour Lenin."* It was followed by what sounded like numbers, also in Russian, coming five digits at a time.

Since the FBI agents manning the earphones didn't speak Russian, they were unable to make sense of the broadcast—but they thought this could be a message for Thompson beamed from either the Soviet Union or an Iron Curtain country.

To the G-men, *"Amour Lenin"* meant nothing. Translated literally it was "Love Lenin." Even with the numbers, it made no sense. Undoubtedly it was code. The only way the agents could find out what the broadcast was about was to break the code.

Although their cryptographic experts had broken many codes—particularly during World War II and the Korean conflict—the FBI's ingenious technicians couldn't crack this one. They only had this brief message and three other short ones that came over the radio during the next several weeks; not enough to decipher the code.

But the FBI agents on stakeout noticed that after each message Thompson was spurred into action, although even those movements didn't always appear consistent. Four days after the first broadcast, the G-men observed a car following the airman as he was driving from the base to his trailer at the end of a tour of duty. A woman was behind the wheel. As Thompson pulled into the camp, the other car just drove past and kept going. The FBI men dismissed the incident as an unrelated occurrence.

The next night, however, they spotted the same woman and car following Thompson. This time, as the airman approached the trailer camp, the girl behind the wheel began honking her horn urgently. Thompson finally stopped, got out, and walked to the other car, which had pulled up behind him. They spoke a few seconds, then Thompson got into his car and drove off. The woman followed. So did the G-men, at a safe distance.

They tailed the two autos to an isolated area on the fringe of Malmstrom's airstrip and watched from afar when the cars stopped. Thompson got out of his station wagon, walked to the other car, got in beside the driver, and—in the reflection of his own taillights glowing through the windshield—the G-men saw the two embracing. Then for the next half hour the couple just sat talking. Finally, Thompson got out, returned to his car, and drove back to the trailer camp. The woman also left in her car, followed by two FBI agents. She drove across the Missouri River into Great Falls.

The G-men saw her park and go into a tavern. A short time later they spotted her—behind the bar. She was a barmaid there. Now she'd bear watching, too.

For the next few days, Thompson did nothing unusual. Then one night his watchers tailed his station wagon on a long trip into Minnesota which concluded at a bar and grill in Minneapolis. Thompson went to the bar, ordered a beer, stayed a while, then left.

The G-men noticed Thompson following a man who had left the tavern just before him. The airman stalked his quarry for several blocks to an old apartment house. When the man went inside, Thompson walked up a short flight of steps to the lobby, looked inside at the mailboxes, then came out, hurried back to his station wagon, and drove home.

Three weeks later, on a Saturday afternoon, Thompson again made the long journey to Minneapolis. This time he visited a library where G-man saw him checking through newspaper files. After some twenty minutes, he seemed to find what he was looking for, studied the item for a minute or so, made a note on a piece of paper, and left for his trailer camp.

By late July, 1958, the FBI had a thick file on Robert Glenn Thompson's activities. There were many entries which had all the earmarks of an espionage agent's movements—but, as yet, no specific act of treason had become apparent.

The FBI, however, was not about to write off Thompson. There were just too many suspicious and inexplicable factors involving him.

Why did Thompson tune in on the Russian short-wave broadcast?

Why did he rendezvous with the barmaid—and how did she figure in the spy plot, if indeed there was a plot?

Who was the man he trailed in Minneapolis—and why did Thompson go back and check the newspapers at the library?

All these questions, and more, still haunted the FBI. And soon another puzzling development added to the enigma. Thompson responded to a call for volunteers to serve at the Air Force base in Goose Bay, Labrador.

Thompson received his transfer in late August and headed for his new post, after first bringing his pregnant wife, baby, dog, and their possessions back to Detroit. This time the family moved in with Thompson's mother.

At Goose Bay, Thompson fell into the routine of his clerical duties and never once betrayed a movement that suggested espionage. He never strayed far from the post and was never seen making contact with anyone.

But then Thompson suddenly aroused curiosity once more—when he put in for a discharge!

By December, the papers came through and he was honorably discharged. He headed straight for his mother's home in Detroit.

For the next two weeks, Thompson's movements were watched, but fanned no suspicion. Then, on January 14, a man who seemed to be in his middle or late thirties came to the house. There was nothing distinctive about him except that he walked stiffly erect with an almost military bearing, and his clothing had a distinctively European styling.

Within minutes, the visitor emerged with Thompson and they walked together to a nearby restaurant and huddled in a conversation of whispers for the better part of an hour. Sometimes they spoke heatedly, but always in quiet tones. The stranger seemed disturbed now and then with what Thompson was saying. Finally, they got up, left the restaurant, and parted with a firm handshake. Thompson went home while the stranger went to board a Pennsylvania Railroad train.

The FBI man who got on the train with him had an unexpectedly long ride—all the way to Washington, D. C. At the end of the trip, however, the agent was not surprised to find his prey's path took him straight to the Soviet Embassy.

After this it was just a matter of developing negatives that were shot of the meeting in the Detroit restaurant and on the street when Thompson and the stranger shook hands, to tell the FBI that the stranger was quite well-known in diplomatic circles in the capital.

He was none other than Boris Vladimorovich Karpovich, the Soviet Embassy's information counselor.

With a man of Karpovich's stature dealing with Thompson, it was logical to assume the Russians were after something specific— perhaps something very big. So far the FBI had not been able to determine what Thompson had been doing for the Soviet Union.

But with Karpovich in the picture, the FBI reasoned, things would begin to happen. And before very long they did.

Thompson's unshakable FBI shadows found him making inquiries in the Detroit area about certain people. One was a prisoner in the state penitentiary in Milan, not far from the motor capital. The other was a patrolman on the Detroit police force. Thompson worked like a professional investigator. For example, he went to the policeman's neighbors and, showing them credentials that identified him as an insurance company investigator, asked for background on the cop—information about his financial status, his drinking habits, his moral standards.

There was no clear reason for these inquiries except that the Russians might have been trying to discover weaknesses that could be exploited, with an eye to recruiting the prisoner and the policeman as Soviet spies.

On March 6, 1959, the FBI in Washington sent a teletype message to the Bureau in Detroit advising agents that Boris Karpovich had just boarded a flight at Washington National Airport—for Detroit.

There was no need to have an agent on the plane. But FBI men were on the scene when the Russian landed in Detroit and they didn't have to do much guessing about Karpovich's mission. He had a date with Thompson.

The Russian and Thompson met in front of the Fox Theater, walked along the crowded street, went into a restaurant, had coffee, talked some more, then parted company. Karpovich went to the airport and flew back to Washington.

Two days later Thompson was trailed to a catering place in the Hamtramck section of the city, an area heavily populated by persons of Polish descent. His only interest, it seemed to the two G-men who followed him, was in taking pictures with his 35-mm camera at a wedding reception there. The photos were of the older people at the party.

The FBI's only conclusion from this activity again was that the Russians in Washington were perhaps seeking to recruit agents—and the pictures would serve to tell them which of the people (they were of both Polish and Russian descent, or actually immigrants from those countries) could be linked with relatives in the old country and thus be blackmailed.

Toward the last days of summer, Thompson apparently became aware of one of the simple realities of civilian life, a thing called employment. He hadn't worked since he was let out of the Air Force the previous December. So now, in late October, he went to work for a chemical plant in Detroit. His salary: seventy-seven dollars a week.

In the next eleven months, Thompson was watched closely, but his movements were not far different from those that had been catalogued thus far. He went to the public library on several occasions and appeared to do research in the newspaper files. He visited various homes in the city, and the suburbs on other occasions. He also dropped in at some bars, met persons the FBI recorded but couldn't identify. All in all he appeared to be busy doing something —yet exactly what wasn't clear.

But something did become clear on June 23, 1961, which the FBI recorded as the second most significant date in its now-bulging file on Robert Glenn Thompson, suspected spy.

Thompson had suffered severe burns in an accident at the chemical plant and gone through a long period of convalescence. Then he quit his job and opened a small auto body-repair shop which he called Robert Thompson and Son.

During this period, too, Mrs. Thompson became pregnant again and gave birth to a son, their third child. She had borne a daughter in her previous pregnancy, the one that had hospitalized her while the Thompsons were still in Montana. So that made two girls and a son for the couple.

The June 23rd incident was a meeting with a slender, youthful-looking man with curly black hair, wearing a suit conspicuously styled in the sedate Soviet cut, who stopped at Thompson's house. The G-men saw Mrs. Thompson escort the visitor to her husband's auto repair shop, where he was greeted by Thompson as someone he knew.

In the next few days, Thompson spent a lot of time in the man's company. They went to various places together, but none seemed as important as the two stops that they made on the last day of the visitor's stay in Detroit. Both of these stops were the area's Nike missile sites.

It was obvious to the FBI observers what the stranger was after —pictures of the Detroit defense positions against air attack. To throw off suspicion, the photo-taking mission was camouflaged with a gimmick—each picture the man snapped was of Thompson posing with a tourist-like smile. But it didn't fool the G-men. They could see that every photo was taken with an ample background of the missile site.

Afterward, Thompson drove the man to the airport and a New York-bound plane. The FBI sent a teletype message that Fedor Kudashkin was on his way back.

How did the FBI know who the man was?

He had been captured in the sights of the G-men's telephoto lens on his first day in Detroit, at Thompson's shop. The negative was developed in the FBI's photo lab there and flown to Washington. It was just a matter of an hour or so before the face was identified from file pictures on the Soviet diplomatic corps.

Kudashkin was chief of translators for the Soviet Mission to the U.N. Once again this pointed up the FBI's contention that the operations of Soviet agents in the United States are inseparably linked to both Russian diplomatic bases, in New York and Washington.

Kudashkin revisited Detroit in mid-August, 1961, spent a day with Thompson, then went back to New York. Several days later, Thompson drove away from his shop in a beat-up pickup truck and followed U.S. Highway 25 out to the intersection of Telegraph Road. He parked on the shoulder of the highway and sat behind the wheel for nearly an hour, apparently waiting for someone—or something.

Shortly before eleven A.M. it became obvious why he was there when an Army jeep hove into view in the distance, its headlights burning despite the brilliant sunlight. The jeep was escorting a truck. The truck was pulling a long, narrow, round object.

It was a one-hundred-foot missile.

As the FBI men watched through field glasses and recorded the scene with cameras, Thompson took pictures with his own camera from the cab of his truck. When the missile caravan had passed, he made a U-turn and drove back to his shop.

Two weeks later, Thompson and his wife were spotted leaving their house with luggage. They got into a 1960 red Oldsmobile sedan which the former airman was now driving, and they headed on what looked like a long trip. And it was—it took them to Long Island, then to Washington, and finally back home. They were gone ten days. During his stay in Washington, his FBI tail watched Thompson meet Boris Karpovich briefly a block from the Soviet Embassy.

From its investigation, the FBI concluded that aside from espionage, Thompson was looking for a home as well as for a business to buy on Long Island. He had made inquiries about renting a residence in the huge Levittown development on the Island and had put a twenty-five dollar binder on a Cape Cod bungalow. He had also negotiated in a tentative way with the owner of a body-and-fender shop in the Copiague area farther east on the Island.

Two weeks later, on Friday, September 7, Thompson loaded his wife and children into the car and headed East once more. This time it looked permanent. A moving van had been loaded up with the family's furniture and possessions earlier and had started eastward. The Thompsons were moving to Levittown.

The next morning, Saturday, Thompson deposited his family in their new home. Then he left quickly on a forty-mile drive, over the Bronx-Whitestone Bridge from Long Island to the Bronx and along the Hutchinson River Parkway into Westchester County. His trail led to the station of the New York, New Haven and Hartford Railroad in Rye. Thompson pulled into the railroad parking lot, which on a Saturday afternoon was nearly empty, and walked to the eastbound platform.

Shortly after three P.M. a commuter train from Grand Central Terminal in New York City pulled into the station. A handful of passengers alighted, one of whom the FBI recognized—Fedor Kudashkin, the Soviet's man in the U.N.

Kudashkin approached Thompson in the waiting room. They shook hands, then sat on a bench and began talking. At times it seemed the Russian was angry. Occasionally he shook his finger at Thompson.

Finally, after twenty-five minutes, the conversation ended seemingly on a friendly note. Kudashkin left the waiting room first, walked to the westbound platform, and minutes later boarded the Stamford-to-New York local for Grand Central. Thompson drove home to Levittown.

Just when the FBI had settled down on its stakeout of Thompson's home, conveniently with agents from its nearby offices in

Mineola, it had to pull up stakes because he moved again. He took a residence in Copiague, where he had landed a job as a subcontractor servicing oil burners for a local fuel distributor.

For the next five months the FBI found no unusual activity. Then in mid-January, 1962, the G-men spotted Kudashkin with a shorter, thinner man, pulling up in front of Thompson's house. Thompson himself admitted them. After some twenty minutes the visitors left.

There was no doubt, as far as the FBI was concerned, that Thompson was still mixed up in some phase of subversion. But what?

As the agents continued to shadow Thompson they observed more meetings, sometimes in the open, sometimes cloaked with deceptive movements which the G-men were convinced were efforts by the Communists to detect whether Thompson was being followed.

One such cloak-and-dagger rendezvous was observed on the third Saturday in February, 1962, in the Bronx. Thompson drove his red Oldsmobile to the Gun Hill Road section, parked on the street, then walked to Jerome Avenue. There, under the Mosholu Parkway elevated station of the IRT's Lexington Avenue-Woodlawn Road subway line, he went into a bar and grill.

After having two beers he left and strolled along a circuitous path for fifteen minutes, through a number of side streets off Jerome Avenue, almost in a cloverleaf pattern, or squared-off figure eight, with Jerome Avenue always the pivot. After stopping in a luncheonette, Thompson walked along more of this route, finally stopping in front of a men's clothing store on the west side of Jerome.

In fact, during the hour of aimless walking, someone—not Kudashkin—was probably watching to see if Thompson was being followed. But the FBI didn't have to chase after Thompson. They had seven agents in the vicinity and they hardly had to step away from their posts. Thompson was never out of an agent's sight.

Thompson and Kudashkin spoke for about fifteen minutes in front of the clothing store, then parted. Kudashkin returned to the Soviet Mission of the United Nations; Thompson went home to Copiague.

Toward the end of June, 1962, Thompson and his family again moved, this time to Bay Shore, Long Island, where it looked as though they might stay. They bought a modest Cape Cod bungalow with a finished attic and basement, in a row of similar homes at 1693 North Gardiner Drive.

Why, no one could say, but Thompson painted the exterior shingles a bright barn red. All the other homes in the block were white.

Thompson also set himself up in his own business in Bay Shore, calling it the Best Fuel Oil Service. He started with one delivery truck, then bought others. Eventually he also took over a gasoline station in Babylon.

He was doing well. The FBI now had to wonder whether Thompson's suspected activities as a spy were responsible for the financial wherewithal that enabled him to advance so rapidly in business. He would bear more watching.

In the weeks and months ahead it became clear what Thompson's duties on Long Island were for the Soviet spy network. The FBI observed him again and again near oil and gasoline storage tanks, water filtering plants, chemical plants, the gas storage tanks of the Long Island Lighting Company and the Consolidated Edison Company in Queens and other boroughs of New York City—all ideal targets for sabotage if the Soviet Union ever decided to unleash a wave of terror against the United States.

As it was learned later, the information—and the photos—that Thompson was obtaining were going into the master plan to blow up key military, industrial, and other resources along the Eastern Seaboard and imperil the lives of millions. The plot was part of a Cuban wave of terror designed by the Kremlin and which, instead, blew up on the perpetrators on November 17, 1962, when the FBI moved in and arrested the conspirators.

But Thompson was not apprehended at that time, for he was not directly linked to the plot. He was merely supplying information to the conspirators.

The FBI knew exactly how he did it. Thompson drove to the various key installations in an old panel truck. He had rigged up his 35-mm. camera to the small window on the right panel wall, and with a ten-foot-long cable that extended from the shutter to the ceiling over the driver's seat, Thompson snapped pictures of vital installations at will.

Thompson must have felt extremely secure in his work for the Soviet Union. He exhibited more gall than any suspected spy the FBI had ever pursued.

Perhaps his boldest venture, the FBI says, was his attempt on the night of February 23, 1963, to "case" the Bureau's office in Babylon, Long Island. As a rule, the office is closed at night, even though agents may be at work. In fact, two agents from that very office were the "tail" on Thompson that night.

The G-men followed their quarry back to their own headquarters and watched incredulously as Thompson scaled a fire escape to the second floor and peeked inside. They weren't certain what he would do. Then it seemed to become clear; after Thompson had spent about five minutes looking into the office—a night light was burning inside—he climbed down and drove home.

He had familiarized himself with the layout. Conceivably, the Soviets were thinking about bugging the office.

The watch on the former GI continued uninterruptedly through the spring and into the summer of 1963. By now the dossier on Robert Glenn Thompson was bulging. Every step, every move he made had been watched and recorded by the FBI.

His rendezvous with Kudashkin had become a ritual. They would meet almost anywhere two people might be expected to meet, without betraying the slightest apprehension about being watched. They were seen at literally scores of restaurants, at stations of the Long Island Railroad's South Shore line, and numerous other locales that provided little or no privacy.

The FBI was thoroughly familiar with the modus operandi by now. Kudashkin was assigning Thompson to gather the information and photos about the gasoline, oil, and gas storage tanks, and the other vital installations on Long Island; Thompson was delivering that information and photos. And almost certainly he was being paid for his services.

The FBI knew this not only from its visual observations, but also from what it picked up on its listening posts. The agents had put taps on Thompson's phone at home and his place of business. Both places of business, actually, for Thompson had by this time expanded his operations and opened another gas station and auto body-repair shop in Bay Shore. He was doing very well indeed.

But there was a disturbing development on August 14, 1963, which the FBI couldn't explain. Without evident reason, Kudashkin was suddenly ordered back to Moscow by his superiors. Since the United States had made no formal complaint against the Soviet spy, it had to be assumed the Russians either felt that Kudashkin's work was finished or that he was suspected by the FBI. Playboy, bon vivant, good-time Charlie, Kudashkin's free-wheeling ways had gotten him into hot water on at least one occasion.

In 1959, on a hot August night, Kudashkin, then a secretary with the Soviet Mission to the U.N. and its top public information officer, had gone to Playland Amusement Park in Rye Beach, for a fling, accompanied by Igor Ivanovich Andreev, also a secretary with the Mission.

The park was closed, for it was after one A.M., but Kudashkin and Andreev thought they could get in past the locked gates. They sang and shouted so loudly that the Rye town police had to come and take them away. It was evident to the cops that the two Soviet disturbers of the peace were drunk.

But Kudashkin and Andreev weren't detained long at the station house. They simply produced their diplomatic credentials and no charges were lodged against them.

On the face of it, the Russians would seem to have taken ultimate reprisals against Kudashkin, because late the following year they removed him from his secretary's post and put him into the translator's job. At least that's how some diplomatic observers at the U.N. explained it at the time.

But the FBI knew better. Kudashkin had been given his new assignment only so that he could work with Thompson. His duties as a Mission secretary wouldn't have allowed the freedom of movement the lesser job permitted. Moreover, the Soviets were protecting themselves. If Kudashkin were caught, it would look better if he were a lower echelon employee.

With Kudashkin gone, the FBI kept an eye out for Thompson's next Soviet contact. But they went through the winter and into the spring of 1964 without any indication that a new intermediary had been assigned to Thompson.

By July 20, 1964, when the G-men were unable to detect any further direct association with Soviet agents, an order was issued by John J. Malone, the agent in charge of the New York office, to pick up Thompson for questioning.

The approach was subtle. The FBI didn't want to frighten Thompson—or scare off the Russians. The plan was to win Thompson over, to extract all possible information on his activities, and to retain him as a kind of counterspy for future espionage assignments the Reds might give him.

Two FBI agents waited near Thompson's home on the night of July 20. When they saw him returning behind the wheel of one of his trucks, the agents drove up to the house and identified themselves.

"We want to ask you some questions," one told him.

"Not here," Thompson pleaded.

The agents escorted him into their car and drove to another part of the neighborhood.

"We know what you've been doing," one of the agents said. "Do you want to tell us about it?"

Thompson brooded over the question.

"Yeah," he finally said. He almost seemed relieved.

Then it began, the exhaustive interrogation which would give the FBI chapter and verse of Thompson's espionage activities, a lurid tale that began in West Berlin nearly seven years before. The full story wasn't told in the first brief meeting.

There were scores of meetings—in restaurants, bars, parking lots, railroad stations—just about any place suitable for conversation. In fact, the routine was strikingly similar to the system used by the Soviet espionage agents. The FBI didn't want Thompson to be spotted talking with its agents any more than the Reds wanted him seen talking with theirs.

Over the remaining months of 1964, Thompson was questioned without letup. Piece by piece, he told the whole shocking tale.

"I had no idea why the Air Force assigned me to the OSI in Berlin. I had no training and certainly I wasn't anxious for it. But they gave me the job and put me into the investigation unit's file room. What's more, they put me in charge of it. And I wasn't even a high school grad.

"I wasn't in the job very long before I became disgusted with the methods the OSI was using to recruit East and West Germans into our counterintelligence system. We'd send girls to some of the big shots to have an affair with them so we could blackmail them for information. It was real dirty stuff.

"Then I began to drink to get my mind off the things that were bugging me. I never drank much before when I was in the States. I got into a few minor jams as a result and I decided I'd better let up.

"Then I met my wife, Evelyn. I saw her in a plumbing shop and

I went in and asked her directions back to Tempelhof Air Base because I was lost. She told me how to get there. When I left I got to thinking that she was an attractive girl and that I could go for her.

"So I called her up at the plumbing shop and got her to go with me on a date. We went together for about three months and I asked her to marry me. She said okay, but it was almost ten months before the Air Force gave their okay. You have to get their permission to marry a German girl when you're in the OSI.

"I let up on my drinking after we were married and I settled down as a happily married man. But then one day, after Evelyn had our first baby, I got word from home that my grandfather died. I went to the colonel I worked for and asked him if I could get a furlough to attend the funeral. He turned me down flat. He said he couldn't spare me. That was a joke. I could never do anything right for him, but he couldn't spare me. That made me very angry—and bitter.

"It made me start drinking again and it started me and Evelyn to quarreling. I used to be in some lousy moods as a result of my drinking. I was in a particularly lousy mood one Sunday afternoon at the base, and when another airman came and asked me to go downstairs to the noncoms' club for a few drinks, I went. This got me soused and when the guy asked me to go into Berlin for more drinks, I went with him.

"I took off my jacket in the bar and when I went to put it on later my gun, a .38-caliber Smith and Wesson, was missing. So when I got back to the base I went to the supply warehouse and lifted another gun for myself. The next morning some guys turned in the gun I lost to the colonel. He called me in—and there I stood with the gun I had stolen in my holster. He wanted to know how it was I had two guns. I had to tell him the truth.

"That led to a court-martial. I pleaded guilty, naturally, and they busted me from first class airman. They took away my privileges and restricted me to the post. They told me I had to send my wife and kid back to the States. I was bitter about having to send them home to live in Detroit. But I had to do it.

"After they left, I was very disgusted and bitter; I'd go from day to day not talking to anybody or seeing anybody. I began looking for a way to occupy my mind, so I started counting the holes in the office ceiling tiles. On most counts I got 11,871 holes. Sometimes I'd get a different count, more or less, and I'd start to count all over again.

"While I was on one of my binges I met a German girl, a real good-looking dish, and started shacking up with her. I began to tell her my troubles and she finally asked me why don't I do something about it. So I decided maybe I should—I'd defect to the East Germans.

"What had really put me over the cliff was the colonel. He was always down on me, but this particular day he really laced into me for being in civilian clothes and needing a shave. I blew my stack and said to hell with him. I went back to the barracks, shaved, had a few drinks, and went out. I had decided to get even with the colonel and the whole damn Air Force.

"I called the East Berlin police and told them what I had in mind, that I wanted to come over to their side. They told me to wait at the phone booth and pretty soon one of them came over and took me across the border. When we got to their headquarters I told them I wanted political asylum. But they wouldn't give it to me.

"The cops had taken me to Soviet agents who questioned me at length. They kept telling me they believed I was a counterspy. They told me I'd have to go back, but they let me sleep in East Berlin that night. The next morning I returned to my base.

"A few nights later I was walking along a street when a limousine pulled up and someone called my name. He invited me into the car, told me his name was Steven, and that I was wanted across the border. I got in and was driven into East Germany.

"They questioned me again, took my picture, then asked me for my identification papers which they kept. They told me that I was now working for them—as a spy. And if I wouldn't, they'd expose me as one to the authorities in West Berlin.

"I was struck with fear. I didn't want to get into espionage, but they had me. Not only that, but there was my wife and baby. They told me they knew all about my wife's family—her grandparents, some uncles, and few aunts were living in East Germany. They told me to cooperate—or else.

"So I agreed to work for them. They gave me twelve dollars and fifty cents and a miniature camera to photograph secret documents. They said they wanted anything I could get my hands on.

"At first I didn't take any photos, but then my colonel got me mad again and I started taking shots of documents that concerned investigations we had undertaken on people, and occasionally the Berlin police blotter.

"At times I photographed reports on essential elements of information clipped from newspapers and magazines and political and economic information that had nothing to do with the defense of the United States. I was selective and didn't photograph anything that would hurt the United States.

"I got them into East Berlin without much trouble—there was no wall then. And it wasn't hard to hide the two rolls of film, which had about fifty shots each. I simply slipped them into the lining of my European sport coat. No one bothered to search me the first time or any other time after that.

"My handlers in East Berlin didn't comment much at first on the documents I was photographing. But as time passed they seemed to be more and more interested in what I was getting for them.

"I'd give them fifty to one hundred documents every two weeks for about three months. Once in a while they'd give me money, usually twelve dollars and fifty cents.

"I wasn't in it for money. I was disgusted and it was part of my plan to get revenge.

"Then when I got my orders to ship back to the States, I went and told them in East Berlin. The news shook them up and got them excited. They calmed down after a while and said they'd arrange for me to meet one of their agents in Canada, in Smith Falls, Ontario, in front of a movie house at one P.M. on the first Sunday of any month.

"They gave me one thousand dollars and told me to buy a short-wave radio and to tune in on a special part of the band and listen for the code words *'Amour y Lena'* (not *Amour Lenin* as the FBI first believed). The code was followed by a series of messages, also in code.

"They also gave me a distinctive cigarette lighter with four playing cards, all aces, on its face. They told me my contact in Canada would have a matching lighter.

"And they gave me a password. It was a question and answer. The question was: 'Are you from Toledo, Ohio?' The answer I was supposed to give was: 'Yes, since June 23, 1932.'

"They also gave me secret writing paper. I was to use a stylus to write an invisible message in code. I'd write a cover letter over the invisible message and send it off to an address in Helsinki, Finland.

"Oh yeah—another thing they gave me was a flashlight containing a battery that came apart. It was equipped to photograph an eight-and-a-half-by-ten sheet of paper into a dot as big as a period at the end of a sentence. I was told to insert the dot between a split postcard, re-glue the card, and mail it to Helsinki.

"About a week before I left Berlin for the States, the Soviets asked me to get a five-day pass. They said they had something important for me to do in the East. I got the pass and went into East Berlin. They then put me on a huge plane, real plush, and they flew me to a resort place on the Black Sea. This was inside Russia.

"I don't remember the name of the place, but I was there five days. They put me through a rugged course, training me in how to use radio equipment and the Russian language, particularly in the reading of ciphers.

"Then some agents asked me to embed a radio transmitter in the wall of the OSI office when I got back. At first I didn't want to do it. Later I changed my mind and I put the transmitter in one of the walls.

"Right after that they sent me to Malmstrom. I stopped off in Detroit to pick up my wife and baby; then we drove to my new post.

"While I was in Malmstrom I had one written contact with the Soviets. I used the secret paper to tell them where I was stationed. But I never kept that appointment in Canada. Neither did I use any of the other equipment they gave me, because by that time I realized I had made a terrible mistake and I just wanted to get away from them.

"At one time I even considered suicide to get out of the mess. I went to a motel in Billings. I was going to kill myself, blow out my brains with a shotgun—honest. But I didn't have the courage, I suppose.

"I began to worry that a Soviet agent would try to approach me with a demand for secret information. The only person who actually contacted me while I was at Malmstrom was a girl named Virginia—whom I had met in spy school. I was surprised to find that she was there, working as a barmaid in Great Falls. But we didn't do any business. I think she was just checking up on me to make certain I was around. [The FBI is aware of Virginia and at last report knew exactly what she was doing.]

"Then I decided to get out of the whole thing. They were asking for volunteers to serve in Goose Bay, Labrador, and I put in for a transfer. When I got it, I sent my wife and children back to Detroit to stay with my mother. Then at the end of 1958 I was discharged and I went back to Detroit.

"No sooner did I get back than I learned that a man had been around looking for me. He came back sometime later and told me he was John Kurlinsky. [The FBI said this man actually was Boris Karpovich, the counselor of the Soviet Embassy in Washington.]

"Kurlinsky wanted me to go back to the Air Force or the Army to get more information. One time he even asked me to get a job with the FBI in Detroit. I stalled him. Then they left me alone for two years, until the summer of 1961.

"Then a man I know only as Gregor [Fedor Kudashkin of the Soviet Mission to the UN] came to my home. He pressed me to get information for them. I told him I couldn't do it because I was unable to get jobs of a security nature.

"I decided I'd better get out of Detroit to escape further meetings with Soviet agents. That's when I moved to Long Island. We stayed in Levittown for a month, then went to Copiague. I purposely left no forwarding address at Levittown, but the Russians trailed me and found me.

"Gregor was the guy who came to my house with another Soviet agent whose name I never got. Gregor said he had spent several days in my neighborhood trying to locate me. How he knew I was in Copiague, Gregor said, was that he got my mother to tell him. He said he had to drive around until he found my red Oldsmobile with Michigan license plates.

"There was no way out for me, so I had to continue to work for them. They wanted information about water reservoirs on Long Island, on the gas lines between New York and Long Island, and on power plants in the area. They also wanted information about gas storage tanks, oil tanks, and other facilities.

"They also instructed me to shoot pictures.

"One time Gregor gave me a list of names of people living in Nassau, Suffolk, Queens, and New Jersey. These people are agents of the Soviet Union. Some are active, but most of them are sleepers. Gregor wanted information about where they lived, their jobs, and their financial status.

"I didn't like doing that because one time when I had to do something like that in Minneapolis, I found out the guy I gave information on was suddenly dead."

The FBI said this explained Thompson's two trips to Minneapolis. The first to get information on the man, the second to check the newspaper obits to see if his name was there. It was. Officially, the man died of "natural causes" and there was no proof that Soviet agents were responsible for his death.

At a later time, Thompson informed the FBI he believed the Russians killed the Minneapolis man with a "secret kind of poison that cannot be detected unless you look for it in the autopsy."

"I was helping Gregor with most of the information he was looking for, because he wasn't asking for anything that involved the security of my country. All of it was common knowledge to anybody," Thompson's confession continued.

"I didn't really do anything bad. I wish I could work for you fellows. There's a lot I could uncover for you . . . I would be real useful as a counterspy."

Thompson eventually went into far greater detail on his espionage activities. He gave the FBI the names of the people he investigated for the Soviets, including the policeman and the prisoner he checked on while still in Detroit. The FBI did not reveal these people's identities or say why the Red agents were looking for information and data on them.

Robert Glenn Thompson's career as a spy for the Soviet Union ended unofficially when the FBI picked him up. But the G-men let him enjoy his freedom for a while to see what other agent or agents —now that Kudashkin had departed—would get in touch with him. For the rest of 1964, the FBI said, the Russians made no visible or detectable effort to communicate with Thompson.

It seemed to the FBI now that Thompson's usefulness to the Kremlin spy network had come to an end.

And so had his freedom.

On January 7, 1965, a Federal grand jury in Brooklyn, after hearing evidence presented by U.S. Attorney John J. Hoey's staff, returned a three-count indictment against Robert Glenn Thompson, charging that he committed acts of espionage against the United States in East and West Berlin, in New York, Michigan, Montana, and in the District of Columbia.

The indictment said specifically that Thompson "did conspire and agree . . . to communicate, deliver, and transmit to the USSR documents, writings, photographs, notes, and information relating to military equipment, installations, missile sites, code books, intelligence and counterintelligence activities, including the identities of Government personnel."

The thirteen "overt acts" accused Thompson of receiving a total of seventeen hundred dollars from the Communists—rather meager pay for the services he had rendered.

The Government also named two co-conspirators in the indictment—Fedor Kudashkin and Boris Vladimorovich Karpovich.

No time was wasted, once Karpovich's name came out in court. The State Department immediately declared the Soviet Embassy man persona non grata and told the Soviet Government to take him back. Within thirty-six hours Boris Karpovich was out of the Soviet Embassy in Washington and on a plane to Moscow—and a rather uncertain future.

There was nothing the United States could do about Kudashkin. The Soviet Union had taken care of him, at least in getting him out of this country before the plot blew up. Then, too, Kudashkin's future had no particularly bright rays. In the Communist world, a spy who fails is the worst kind of failure.

After Robert Glenn Thompson's arraignment in Brooklyn Federal Court, he was released in fifteen thousand dollars bail to await trial. The trial was ordered because Thompson pleaded not guilty.

Judge Walter Bruchhausen at first entertained the plea of the U.S. Attorney's office to set bail at twenty-five thousand dollars, on the grounds that Thompson's crime, if proved, could bring the maximum penalty for espionage against his own country—execution.

But attorney Sidney Siben, of Bay Shore, pleaded with the court to release Thompson. Siben said, "Thompson knew he was under investigation, having been questioned as long as a year ago." The lawyer was trying to show that Thompson wouldn't try to get away, inasmuch as he had the fuel oil business and other business including real estate investments.

"If he is held in jail because of inability to make bail, his wife will be unable to maintain the business and they will go broke," the lawyer pleaded.

Lower bail was then set and a professional bondsman put up the fifteen thousand dollars.

Thompson was released. He left with his wife, who had come to court for the proceedings. Outside the courtroom he was besieged by the press. Thompson categorically denied all the charges.

Meanwhile, some of his neighbors in Bay Shore were stunned by the news of his arrest as a spy. They said Thompson was incapable of committing a crime, no matter how small. Certainly he couldn't have engaged in something so conscienceless as espionage.

Other neighbors recalled that Thompson at times had acted brutally toward a next-door neighbor who was a Negro. Thompson was accused of putting a sign out in front of his house which read: "House for Sale—Mixed Neighborhood." He also was accused by his neighbors of hanging a noose from the attic window facing the neighbor's house.

All in all, the reaction in Thompson's community was mixed. His employees also apparently took his arrest with mixed feelings —half of them quit on the spot.

For all of his pleas of innocence, Robert Glenn Thompson was finally to find that he couldn't continue the ruse any longer. He had given the FBI more than twenty statements, and had signed each of them. He had admitted, privately, but officially, to the FBI that he was a spy.

So on March 8, 1965, Thompson was returned to the United States Courthouse in Brooklyn. He stood before Judge Leo Rayfiel in a nearly empty courtroom. He glanced at his wife, who was in a front-row seat, then faced the bench.

The judge read the charge:

"That from, in, or about June, 1957, and continuously thereafter . . ."

"I plead guilty," Robert Glenn Thompson said in a soft voice, when the judge had finished.

He was released in the same fifteen thousand dollars bail and ordered to return May 13 for sentencing.

Outside court, Thompson once again made a statement in solemn tones: "I want to take what I've got coming to me. It's the best thing to do. I've got children to think about . . . I made a big mistake. But remember, I was very young—only twenty-two."

On May 13, Thompson again took his place before the bench. Judge Walter Bruchhausen again presided.

"This court," the judge said, "is confronted with one of the most difficult decisions facing any court. The defendant was engaged during a period of six years, here and abroad, in undermining our national security.

"The consequences thereof are readily determinable. It is clear that his criminal activities warrant severe punishment . . ."

The judge then passed sentence—thirty years.

Thompson, who could have received the death penalty or been imprisoned for life, turned to look at his family in the back of the courtroom. He saw his mother and stepfather and he saw his wife. He tried to wave to them, but there was no recognition from them.

Mrs. Thompson was asked if she wanted to visit her husband in the detention pen, before he was taken to prison.

"I don't want to see him," she said, lowering her head. Then she walked away.

Robert Glenn Thompson, a man who betrayed his own country for the Communists, was now completely forsaken.

He had decided the torrid and perilous game of espionage was not for him and he sought to make amends by offering to become a counterspy . . . but it was too late.

10

A Pentagon Courier Disappears—Another
Bonanza for the Kremlin

"I do not understand," the tearful voice said in English flavored with a thick Austrian accent. "Bob did not say he would miss his work today. I have no idea where he has gone."

Mrs. Robert Lee Johnson was bereft of an explanation about her husband's failure to report to his post at the Pentagon Courier Transfer Station. The forty-three-year-old staff sergeant, a veteran of twenty-two years in the Army, had followed an iron routine each day of the more than five months he had been a dispatchbearer in the capital. He would get out of bed at about ten A.M., wash and shave, eat breakfast, then relax until the early part of the afternoon when he'd have a sandwich or snack. Generally he'd leave his house at 253 Tennessee Avenue in Alexandria around three-thirty P.M. and drive along the pleasant residential streets onto busy U.S. 1 to his assigned space in one of the sprawling parking lots clustered around the Pentagon. At four P.M. he would be "present and accounted for."

His duties at the highly sensitive courier station involved, among other things, the delivery of classified materials between various offices in the Pentagon and the vault where these documents are stored for safekeeping.

On the afternoon of October 2, 1964, Sergeant Robert Lee Johnson had left home as though he were off on another routine four-to-midnight shift, according to what the sergeant's commanding officer could gather over the telephone from Mrs. Johnson.

She said that everything had appeared normal, except for the newly purchased 1965 Chevrolet he was driving.

In the brief telephone conversation with the commanding officer, the missing sergeant's wife seemed unable to speculate about what could have happened to her husband. "He might have had trouble with the car . . . I'm sure he'll come in," she said in a tone mixed awkwardly with embarrassment and uncertainty.

The officer at the Pentagon promised to notify Mrs. Johnson as soon as he heard about her husband. By nightfall, after myriad inquiries and searches, the Army alerted the area's police departments and all provost marshals in the continental United States to be on the lookout for the AWOL soldier.

Not until mid-afternoon of the following day was there a concrete development, which only darkened the mystery. A routine inquiry at the bank where the Johnsons kept their account disclosed a two-thousand-dollar withdrawal the day before. The signature on the voucher was Robert Lee Johnson's.

A flock of questions was raised suddenly. First, how was Johnson able to make the withdrawal if he'd left the house at three-thirty P.M.—since banks close at three P.M.? Mrs. Johnson corrected herself. She said she might have been wrong about the time. Her husband might have left at two-thirty P.M.

She also told authorities there'd been a "disagreement with my husband and he left the house in anger."

The key question in the wake of Johnson's disappearance was whether it was related to his work at the Pentagon. The reply from the Defense Department was crisp but reassuring—an inventory had been made and no classified material was missing from the vault.

A week went by, then a month. Sergeant Robert Lee Johnson's whereabouts continued to baffle authorities. Then on November 8, police in Richmond, Virginia, spotted a car that they suddenly realized had been parked in the same place some time. It looked like it might have been abandoned. A check of the license plate proved it was Johnson's auto.

But where was Johnson?

Not until November 25 did the answer come—from Reno, Nevada, where authorities flashed officials in the East that Staff Sergeant Robert Lee Johnson had just walked into a police station and surrendered himself for being absent without leave from his military duties at the Pentagon.

Army MPs took Johnson in custody and brought him to San Francisco. Weeks later a court-martial found him guilty, reduced him in grade to sergeant, and forfeited his pay for the period of his absence without leave and thirty days more.

Johnson didn't make national headlines, but he did get space in newspapers across the country, even four generous paragraphs in *The New York Times,* which enlightened readers with a bare-bones story of a sergeant who had gone astray, then reappeared.

It wasn't until the following spring, on April 5, 1965, that the meaty part of the story came out from the U.S. Courthouse in Richmond, where a Federal grand jury returned espionage indictments against Sergeant Robert Lee Johnson and a former Army sergeant named James Allen Mintkenbaugh.

How authorities managed to bring the charges against Johnson and Mintkenbaugh has never been explained, although the Justice Department said in its complaint that Johnson began making statements to authorities in December, 1964, a month after he turned himself in as AWOL.

Yet the author has learned that the FBI and military intelligence had definite proof before either Johnson began "spilling his guts" or Mintkenbaugh did his talking, soon afterward.

Authorities never suspected either man up until the time of Johnson's disappearance. Subsequent investigation very quickly brought to light the existence of a far-reaching Soviet spy ring which was operating from West Berlin across the Atlantic as far as Los Angeles. The ring specialized in classified information on United States military installations, missile sites, and intelligence activities.

How the FBI and military intelligence started from scratch on October 2, 1964, the day Johnson disappeared, and in just two months, by the early part of December, 1964, came up with chapter and verse of the spy operation is still a big mystery.

There is a strong suggestion, however, that authorities had some "inside" help—from someone very close to the conspirators.

Here is how the story of espionage involving Johnson and Mintkenbaugh unraveled itself for the author.

It began in 1953, with Johnson a native of Farmingdale, New Jersey. Johnson was a corporal, stationed in the Army's West Berlin Command headquarters. His disposition was bad. He was disgruntled because, among other things, the Army hadn't come through with the promotion to sergeant that he expected.

Sometime in February, he finished his eight-hour day at the base and went home to his wife, the former Hedwig Pipek, an Austrian national whom Johnson married in Vienna in 1949. They then had one son, Robert, born in 1952.

John told Hedwig he was unhappy with the way the Army was treating him and had made up his mind to spy for the Russians to make more money. He asked his wife to get in touch with the Soviets in East Berlin and tell them they could recruit him for espionage. Hedwig assertedly did this and found the Reds receptive.

A week or so later Johnson and his wife crossed over into East Berlin and made contact with the Russians at the Soviet headquarters in Karlhorst. For a price, Johnson consented to provide information about important personages in West Berlin. After he delivered this data, he was introduced to a Soviet intelligence officer, Vitaly Ourjoumov, who gave Johnson instructions on how to use a miniature camera and the way to deliver undeveloped microfilm. The object was to photograph classified documents in the files of the Intelligence Section of the United States Berlin Command. The target was defense secrets dealing with military installations, relative strength of Allied forces stationed in West Germany and other NATO countries, as well as intelligence activities of the United States and its allies.

Since Johnson was assigned to G-2 (intelligence) in the Berlin Command, getting access to the documents was relatively simple. With his Minox miniature, Johnson clicked away at U.S. intelligence documents and smuggled the films off the base each night he left for home. There he'd give them to his wife who, in turn, according to the FBI, would fit them into the hollow heels of shoes the Russians had provided—and walk them across the border to Karlhorst.

This was very profitable work. The Russians put Johnson on the payroll for three hundred dollars a month—almost as much as Uncle Sam was paying him.

Sometime in June or July of 1953, the Russians asked Johnson to find an "assistant" at G-2 to help speed up the operation.

"We must have more microfilms . . . there are many things we want to learn about American intelligence activity . . . we must hurry," Ourjoumov told Johnson. "Get a helper."

Johnson then recruited James Mintkenbaugh for espionage and brought him to Soviet headquarters in Karlhorst. The Soviets immediately gave the two men instruction in the use of secret codes, hollowed-out pencils, microdots, dummy flashlight batteries, and numerous other devices that they could employ to hide and transmit the microfilm negatives.

The two soldiers worked side by side in the theft of U.S. secrets and, at the same time, continued to receive instructions on becoming more proficient in their trade. Their instructor now was a woman whom they knew only as "Paula." Among other tricks, "Paula" taught the two GI spies how to use "contact paper" to write secret messages.

The year 1956 brought the espionage acitivity at G-2 to an end. Johnson and Mintkenbaugh were transferred to the States and discharged because their enlistments were up. Mintkenbaugh, who was mustered out first, in March, received a coded letter from "Paula" a short time later. She wanted him to meet her in West Berlin.

Mintkenbaugh went there, saw "Paula," and was instructed to go to Washington and contact a Soviet agent named "Charles," who would give him his espionage assignments in the future. And "Paula" let Mintkenbaugh know that his prime mission when he returned to the States would be to get in touch with Johnson, who had been discharged in July, prevail upon him to reenlist—and "request duty at one of the missile bases."

Mintkenbaugh came to Washington and met his contact "Charles," a man in his middle thirties who was assigned to the Soviet Embassy. "Charles" instructed Mintkenbaugh to "go after Johnson and tell him we want him to get back in the Army." "Charles" also outlined what the Soviets wanted—photographs and sketches of Nike-Ajax missiles and their bases, photographs of Army missile training manuals, and samples of missile propellant fuel!

As "Charles" laid out the plan, Johnson would obtain the data, pass it to Mintkenbaugh, who would deliver it to "Charles."

Mintkenbaugh caught up with Johnson in Las Vegas, Nevada, explained what the Russians wanted, and found him receptive. Johnson immediately signed up for another hitch and was welcomed back into the Army in February, 1957, with an assignment to a Nike-Ajax site in Los Angeles.

With Mintkenbaugh as his "outside contact," Johnson was able to perform a great deal for the Russians, delivering data almost at will. Mintkenbaugh, who took an apartment in San Martin, developed the microfilm negatives delivered by Johnson at home and brought them, together with other data, to Washington about once a month and turned them over to "Charles."

Johnson, rewarded with promotion to sergeant upon his reenlistment, was never happier than he was in his new work. Not only was he getting the higher pay of his new rank, but also that three hundred dollars a month from the Russians. Mintkenbaugh was drawing a like amount from the Reds.

Johnson photographed all the technical manuals and documents he could get his hands on and snapped every conceivable picture of the physical site, including the missiles, their launchers, and other prohibited and closely guarded installations.

He smuggled the undeveloped negatives out of the base by concealing them at times in his own hollow shoe heels, in the empty battery in his fountain pen flashlight, in the other devices the Russians had taught him to use.

The operation continued without a hitch until April, 1958, when Johnson was transferred to the missile training school at the Air Defense Center at Fort Bliss, Texas.

"Perfect!" cried "Charles" when Mintkenbaugh reported the transfer. "Now we will learn other things. Tell him to continue—we especially want to know what is in the classified manuals at the school."

Johnson not only delivered microfilmed pages of the manuals but also the classified schematic diagrams of the Nike-Ajax missile and numerous other secrets. This espionage activity continued until September, 1959, when Johnson was given a month's furlough to be with his wife as she gave birth to their second child, a daughter named Jessica. Then at the end of his leave Johnson returned to the base to learn he was being transferred to the Army Ordnance Supply Control Agency in Orleans, France.

Once more Mintkenbaugh dashed off to Washington to inform

the Russians about Johnson's transfer. His contact had suddenly been changed. In Charles' place was a chubby man of about forty who went by the very proper Russian name of "Yuri."

"It is good," said Yuri. "There is much we will want to learn about the situation in Orleans."

Mintkenbaugh was instructed to proceed to Orleans and make contact with Johnson. That was in November, 1959. He found the sergeant, his wife, and their two children living in an apartment in the Terminus Hotel.

"They want us to change the operation," Mintkenbaugh told Johnson. "There's going to be a new contact and I'm going to take you to him."

"What are they going to do with you?" Johnson asked.

"They're sending me to Russia—to spy school."

Two days later, Mintkenbaugh returned to the Terminus Hotel and met Johnson and his wife. They went downstairs, got into Johnson's newly purchased car, a Taunus, and drove to Paris near one of the city's so-called cultural theaters.

"I am going to leave you now," Mintkenbaugh said. "Your new contact will be here shortly. His name is 'Viktor.' He'll identify himself. And you will identify yourself by showing him this."

Mintkenbaugh handed the sergeant a five-mark German coin. Then he kissed Hedwig, shook hands with Johnson, and left.

Minutes later, a man of about thirty with a medium build and a youthful, handsome face approached the couple.

"I am 'Viktor,' " he said in English that had only a trace of Soviet accent.

Johnson flashed the German mark. The contact was made. "Viktor" shook hands with the couple, then stepped between them, took them by the arm and escorted them to a nearby café. At the table, "Viktor" was quick to prove his linguistic talent wasn't limited to just one foreign language. The Russian, dressed smartly in the latest continental cut of suit and fashionable broad-collared shirt, engaged the waiters in conversation that revealed an excellent command of French as well. His urbanity blended perfectly into the cosmopolitan Parisian atmosphere.

When "Viktor" finally got down to business, he was deadly serious. He mapped out a series of meetings with Johnson that for the first time exposed the sergeant to the cloak-and-dagger world of espionage he'd known only in movies and television.

"We must be extremely careful," the Russian said quietly. "I will outline the meeting procedures. These will go as follows: you will proceed to a preselected contact point which I will designate in advance. It will most often be a café. I will make visual contact with you.

"Upon recognition, you will walk out of the cafe, turn right, walk down the street and make right turns successively only at intersections. I will then follow a course which will intersect yours. This will allow me ample opportunity to observe the situation at hand."

"Viktor" patted Johnson's hand.

"We don't want to be seen, you understand. That is why we must do it this way."

The Russian then pulled a wad of American money from his pocket and gave it to Johnson—ten twenty-dollar bills.

"This is a Christmas present," he smiled. "Buy your wife a nice gift. And as for your salary, we will continue to pay you three hundred dollars a month."

Johnson plunged into his new assignment with vigor and enthusiasm. Among the priority data the Russians sought from the Ordnance Agency in Orleans were the operations schedules, the size and deployment of the force based at the facility, and details about the Army's antitank missiles being developed and stockpiled there.

By prearrangement, Johnson would meet "Viktor" in the early evening of the first Saturday of each month, almost always in cafés, but never the same one. "Viktor" also seemed to have a rooted dislike for any café with shades or shutters over its windows; thus the rendezvous were held in open-type, airy lounges or bars. As a rule Hedwig accompanied her husband on his encounters with the Russian and would sip coffee and cognac with them while they talked.

"Viktor" would receive any reports or microfilms that Johnson brought, then would question the soldier at length about ordnance operations on which he had not previously sought information. If Johnson was unable to answer about any specific area, he would make certain he was able to at the next get-together.

Meanwhile, the lanky James Allen Mintkenbaugh wasn't being neglected by his Soviet employers by any means. Just as he had told Johnson, the Russians sent him to the Soviet Union for special training in their "school for spies," the Marx-Engels Institute at Gorki. There he was put through the same rigorous course taught native-born Soviet spy candidates, and was instructed in the use of wiretaps, short-wave radio equipment, codes, hidden listening devices, and a variety of other tricks of the espionage trade.

After "graduation," Mintkenbaugh was ordered to Washington where he made contact anew with "Yuri." His assignments now were varied. For example, on some days he would be off pinpointing the location of missile sites in any one of a dozen southwestern states; on other days he'd be up in New York or Ottawa obtaining United States and Canadian birth certificates of persons known to have died. These were to be used by Russian spies in obtaining passports for entry into the two countries.

In the early part of 1961, just when Johnson was again transferred—from Orleans to the Armed Forces Courier Station at Orly Field in Paris—Mintkenbaugh was directed to get a job with a real estate agency in Washington. The purpose was to photograph rental applications of Government employees, to provide the Russians with a record of incomes, backgrounds, and jobs the apartment seekers held. It was inside information which could be invaluable when the Reds sought to recruit new candidates for espionage.

Mintkenbaugh landed a job with the Arledge Realty Company and was put to work in their rental department—just what he wanted. He also rented an apartment in the 6200 block of 28th Street North in Arlington.

Back in Paris, Johnson hit the jackpot. With his previous experience in G-2, he was a logical choice for assignment to the "vault" in the intelligence section at Orly Field. And it turned into a field day for the Russians.

Johnson now had access to all the Confidential, Secret, and Top Secret papers in the classified document vault. But he didn't dare use his Minox miniature. Incongruous as it may seem, it was far simpler for Johnson to remove the documents in their envelopes and take them off the base overnight!

"Viktor" was dumbstruck when Johnson showed up at their first rendezvous after his transfer to Orly Field with a satchelful of classified papers. They met in a café and Johnson put the Air France flight bag in which he was carrying the documents on the table.

"Open it," he smiled to "Viktor."

The Russian pulled the zipper back with a skeptical look. When he saw what was inside, he quickly pulled the zipper closed, shoved the bag back to Johnson with trembling hands, and muttered in a shaky voice, "Come, we must leave immediately."

"Viktor" led Johnson out to the street, hailed a cab, and ordered the driver to take them to an adress on the Rue de Richelieu not far from the Palais Royal. When they got out of the cab, "Viktor" took Johnson by the arm and walked him along the darkened street for what turned out to be a heart-to-heart talk by the experienced spy to the fledgling.

"I don't care what you have done for us in the past," the Russian scolded, "you must never do such a thing again. You must be very careful. Do you realize what you have in the satchel? Suppose someone in the café should have seen? We would be arrested and executed!"

"Viktor" was still trembling, both from fright and from the exhilaration of seeing what Johnson was capable of delivering. Then in staccato instructions he outlined a new procedure which Johnson was to follow when he brought such classified documents out of Orly Field.

He designated "drop" sites around Paris and its outskirts, beginning with one in the countryside, a stone wall adjacent to a small wooden bridge. The wall, about six feet high, had a triangular opening just large enough to receive the airline bag.

"For the time being," the Russian instructed Johnson, "you will bring the material to that wall, place it there, and leave. You will return five hours later and retrieve it. By that time we will have picked it up, photographed the documents, and returned everything in order to the same place."

"Viktor" also designated other "drops" near the same area. One of these additional sites was a large rock near the base of a tree. Johnson was told this one would be used in dire emergency—if he expected to be arrested and was compelled to flee from France. Here he could expect to find instructions, money, and a counterfeit passport with fictitious name.

If on the other hand Johnson felt an emergency meeting was necessary because of some development that would precipitate a change in delivery plans, he was directed to drive to the intersection of the Rue des Pyrénées and the Avenue Gambetta near the Cimetière du Père Lachaise. On approaching this location, Johnson was to flash his headlights twice if he spotted any sign of danger. His Soviet contact ("Viktor" or any other who might be designated in the future) would signal any possible peril by carrying a newspaper in his hand. Thus Johnson and his contact would defer their get-together until a more appropriate time.

A later refinement of emergency meeting procedures took into consideration the advisability of abandoning "drops" in France altogether. In that event, the Soviets would initiate the change by sending Johnson an innocuous-looking letter with an enclosed newspaper clipping that contained a key word indicating a new locale. If the clipping was from a German newspaper, the contact point would be the imposing St. Stephen's Cathedral in Vienna; if a piece of an English language newspaper was in the envelope, the meeting would be held in front of Abraham Lincoln's statue inside the memorial to the Great Emancipator in Washington.

The meetings in Washington were arranged for those occasions when Johnson's duties in the intelligence section at Orly Field periodically took him to the capital on deliveries or pickups of documents at the Pentagon. The dates for these meetings were prearranged, governed by a thirty-day lapse from the date on the newspaper clipping.

Because for one reason or another his Soviet contacts might be changed without notice from time to time, a method of recognition was devised. Johnson would identify himself by carrying a copy of the London *Times,* his Soviet contact by producing a 1921 silver dollar and showing it to Johnson, or simply striking up a conversation that referred to this coin.

Thus "Viktor" established the mechanics of handling the flow of information which Johnson was now certain to produce ever more bountifully. And on that first night when "Viktor" became aware of the gold mine the Soviets had struck at Orly Field, he reached for the airline travel bag that Johnson was carrying with the Air Force documents and said quietly, "I'll take it now . . . I shall return it to you at exactly five A.M. by the cemetery [Père Lachaise] . . . Do not flash your lights this time unless there is danger, and I will not carry a newspaper unless I cannot meet you because we are being watched."

Johnson went to the cemetery location at the appointed hour, met "Viktor," took back the bag with the documents, and returned them safely and unseen to their vault later that morning when he reported to his post. But after this Johnson made all his deliveries to the "drops" that had been designated, alternating between the hole in the wall and the rock, according to instructions given beforehand.

Meanwhile, Johnson continued to meet "Viktor" in different cafés through the summer, fall, and winter of 1961 and on to December 1962. During this time, Johnson also made several trans-Atlantic hops as a courier for the Air Force, and on those occasions rendezvoused with Soviet agents at the Lincoln Memorial—and also had brief reunions with Mintkenbaugh, who was still working as a rental agent for the Washington realty firm and supplying the Russians with, among other things, the names and data of apartment applicants.

Then in December "Viktor" introduced Johnson to another Soviet agent with the code name of "Felix," who seemed to be older, wiser, and more in command of the spy game. Johnson met "Felix" on a rainy afternoon in a wooded area on the outskirts of Paris, and after that it was "Felix" who commanded the espionage activities as they took on bolder proportions.

Now "Felix" brazenly directed Johnson to meet him on a road inside Orly Field at midnight Saturdays, and to bring the documents in the Air France flight bag. "Felix" would take the bag and give Johnson an identical one containing sandwiches and a bottle of cognac.

"Do not drink this liquor," "Felix" warned the sergeant.

He told Johnson that the cognac was laced with a sleep-inducing drug—and he was to offer it to whoever might come along at the wrong time. But the late hour of their get-together invariably provided them with complete privacy. They never encountered an inopportune visitor.

"Felix" would return the airline satchel to Johnson in the same place and the latter would give his Soviet contact the bag that contained the sandwiches and cognac. Then Johnson would return the documents to the vault before daylight.

More precautions were also instituted by "Felix" to put the con-

SURVEYOR ON MOON—
PRIZE FOR RED SPIES

Soviet space scientists were highly impressed when U.S. soft-landed Surveyor I on moon. And well they should have been after Valentin A. Revin, Third Secretary at Russian Embassy, had gotten information about project from American scientist John Huminik, Jr. All wrong information, that is. Huminik was hailed as hero by State Department and Revin was booted back to Moscow.

KREMLIN'S CLAW IN THE CAPITAL

From this imposing mansion (above) which is their embassy in Washington, the Soviet Union directs its espionage agents across the length and breadth of the U.S. But the prime target is only a short distance away across the Potomac—that five-sided immensity, the Pentagon. Army G-2 Colonel William Henry Whalen, aide to the Joint Chiefs of Staff, and Army Sergeant Robert Lee Johnson, a courier, were both caught and convicted of selling Pentagon secrets to Soviets. Major General Sergei Edemski, who while serving as military attaché in Washington was Whalen's contact, is shown (bottom left) after plot was exposed examining military equipment in London.

FAR FROM
THE CONTROVERSY

COLONEL WHALEN

SERGEANT JOHNSON

HANDS-ACROSS-THE-SEA
SPY CASE

At left is tenement at 773 Columbus Avenue where Kurt L. Ponger lived and at right apartment house at 8 West 105th Street which was home for Otto Verber. But after Ponger and Verber became enmeshed in espionage they abandoned Manhattan for Austria, where they worked effectively as spies for Soviet Union until they were caught taking secrets from American military bases. Both were brought back, tried, and convicted. After serving prison sentences, they were deported behind Iron Curtain. In photo below Ponger is shown in custody of FBI agents. Opposite, Verber (left) is comforted by his attorney, Roger Robb, in Federal Court, Washington.

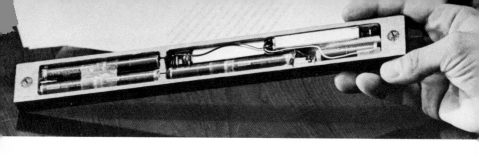

REDS "BUG" STATE DEPARTMENT

This electronic listening device disguised as piece of wood was to be planted in office of Undersecretary of State George C. Ball at direction of two Czechoslovakian diplomats, Jiri Opatrny (left), an attaché, and Zdenek Pisk (right), Second Secretary, both with Czech Embassy in Washington.

Below, hero of the affair, Frank J. Mrkva, a State Department courier, tells reporters about double-agent role he played in foiling plot.

GREETINGS, COMRADE

FBI records for posterity this meeting on the street between Mrkva (left) and Opatrny, one of numerous encounters during many months Czechs were trying to install eavesdropping equipment with very-high-frequency transmitting capability in State Department offices.

YOU CAN'T TELL THEM BY THEIR FACES

In looks, Soviet spies often project typical American image—they can be neighbor-next-door types. Gennadi V. Gavrikov (below), Third Secretary at Russian Embassy in Washington, commanded respectful attention as diplomat—until FBI caught him "cultivating an American writer for role in espionage." At right, John Huminik, Jr. tells House Un-American Activities Subcommittee how Soviet agents tried to steal Surveyor secrets.

spirators at ease after documents were brought back to Johnson. Once he had returned them to the vault, he was directed to drop a crumpled cigarette package at the base of a traffic sign near his home no later than six P.M. Sunday to indicate that all had gone well. If Johnson had encountered trouble, he was to mark the inside of the package with an "X." If no cigarette package was dropped that would indicate serious trouble and the flight plan in which Johnson would find instructions, passport, and money at the rock out in the country would go in effect.

"Felix" also introduced another system of signaling, with modeling clay of different colors, which was to be smeared against a lamp post on one of the desolate fringes of Orly Field. Yellow would mean all was well; red, danger. One night a Paris gendarme caught sight of "Felix" smearing yellow clay on the lamp post and questioned him about his action. "Felix" eluded trouble by feigning drunkenness.

In April of 1964, Johnson was suddenly given another transfer, to be effective May 1. He was advised that it would be to somewhere in the United States. He was not told the specific duty station until the day of his scheduled departure. Johnson drove out to the wall in the country that had been used by him as a drop and drew a "W" with a piece of white chalk.

That meant he was going to be stationed in the Pentagon!

The Soviets were quick to capitalize on the sergeant's new opportunity. Within days after reporting for work at the courier station, Johnson was up to his neck in espionage. But unlike Orly Field, there was no way at the Pentagon to take documents out of the building. However, Johnson had ample opportunity to obtain secrets while on his rounds from the vault to the various offices.

While authorities have refused to discuss to what extent Johnson made good at the Pentagon, there is ample unofficial indication that he did succeed in passing information to the Russians.

One Government source acquainted with the case suggested

that Johnson operated in this fashion. He would report to work, receive a leatherbound dispatch case with classified documents, start on his delivery errand—and en route detour into the nearest men's room, enter a stall, remove the documents, photograph them with his miniature camera, return the papers to the case, and continue to his destination.

He could repeat this routine as often as he was sent on trips with important documents.

In the evening, Johnson would either stop by Mintkenbaugh's apartment on 28th Street in North Arlington, or have him for dinner, to hand over the undeveloped microfilm.

But whatever thefts can be attributed to Johnson and Mintkenbaugh at the Pentagon, their duration was short. The whole operation came to an abrupt halt in October, 1964, when Johnson went AWOL.

Days later, Mintkenbaugh, shaken by Johnson's flight, packed his belongings and headed out to San Martin, California, where he went into hiding. That was where he was picked up by FBI agents after the grand jury handed up the espionage indictments. Johnson was taken in custody as he was making his rounds in the Pentagon, where he had been restored to duty after his court-martial and demotion.

Although they pleaded not guilty to the charges at their hearing on April 15, Johnson and Mintkenbaugh, confronted by overwhelming evidence of their illicit activities, went before Judge Oren R. Lewis in Alexandria's Federal Court on June 7 and changed their pleas to guilty on two counts of *conspiring* in espionage. One count charged them with plotting to gather and sell secret defense information to Russia, the other with acting as Russian agents without notifying the Secretary of State.

Lewis dismissed the espionage charges on a motion by U.S. Attorney C. Vernon Spratley, Jr., who told the court that the Justice Department was satisfied "the ends of justice can be effectively accomplished" by not pursuing the charges which could have resulted in the death penalty.

"There are several problems—the trial is usually protracted and there is great expense involved," declared Spratley.

What he really meant was that there were probably few, if any, solid witnesses against the defendants. For, as the seven-page complaint had indicated, a number of Russians were involved with Johnson and Mintkenbaugh—but all were home free now.

The identity of those Russians was somewhat of a puzzler to the readers of official court papers, for no effort was made to identify them beyond the mere mention of their given or code names. The list contained Viktor, Felix, Voldamar, Mr. Brown, Mr. White, Mr. Schwartz, Nervous Nick, Alex, Charles, Yuri, and Paula.

On July 31, 1965, Johnson and Mintkenbaugh walked into court, stood before Judge Lewis again, and heard pleas in their behalf by their attorneys before sentence was passed.

Mintkenbaugh's attorney, Joseph Forer, told the court that a "psychoneurosis" occasioned by combat duty in two wars (World War II and Korea) had weakened the defendant's will and he was "seduced by professionals" into espionage.

Johnson's attorney, Louis Koutoulakos, said he couldn't explain his client's actions and pleaded with the court to consider the defendant's age and the disgrace that accrued to him and his family after his arrest and exposure.

Forer and Koutoulakos, along with prosecutor Spratley, advised the court that Johnson and Mintkenbaugh had given the FBI a great deal of information about Soviet espionage in this country.

After these statements, Judge Lewis addressed the defendants:

"Our country is not perfect and it never will be. But it's given most of us a good life and I'm sure it's given you gentlemen a good life along with your families.

"I cannot understand why you would be willing to sell your country down the river for a measly bit of pottage."

Then the judge imposed sentence—twenty-five years in Federal prison. That ended the case, but there's an epilogue to the story.

Her husband's disappearance, his subsequent arrest, and the other circumstances evolving from the espionage disclosures were just too much for Johnson's wife. She suffered a nervous breakdown and was confined to a mental institution in Staunton, Virginia. Their children were placed in foster homes.

11

The Army G-2 Colonel—a Paid Red
Spy in the Pentagon

The red brick and green clapboard split-level at 5903 Dewey Drive
is on a tree-lined hilltop street of similar homes which together
make up the portrait of the typical American neighborhood. This
particular neighborhood is in Fairfax County, south of Washington, and perhaps because so many of its residents are in the employ
of the Government, it can hardly do otherwise than mirror the
solid, all-American look.

Apart from the background noise of homeward-bound traffic on
some nearby roads, the wide street, named after the hero of the
Battle of Manila, was empty and quiet. The occupants—Federal
office workers, military personnel, and other civil servants—were
not yet home.

Just before five o'clock on that afternoon of Tuesday, July 12,
1966, an hour when nearby Washington was barely feeling relief
after one of its hottest days of one of its hottest summers on record
—the dreary quiet of Dewey Drive was softly broken.

Six well-dressed men in neatly tailored business suits, clean starched white shirts, and ties carefully knotted against their buttoned collars cruised slowly past the sprawl of cool green lawns and came to a gentle, silent stop at the curb in front of Number 5903.

With precise and hurried steps that seemed practiced, the six strangers left their cars and walked toward the house along the concrete path cutting through the well-tended grass. Three of the men stopped midway up the walk. The other three strode briskly up to the front door.

Inside, the aroma of a roast cooking in the oven was a tempting signal to the occupants that dinner was almost ready. The woman of the house, Bernadine Whalen, was in the kitchen. She had set the table for three—herself, her husband, William, and their eleven-year-old daughter, Kitty.

At this moment, Kitty was sitting with her father in the den watching television, a ritual since the little girl was old enough to appreciate what TV offered.

Life these last five years had been casual for William Henry Whalen, a tall, broad-shouldered, handsome man of fifty-one. He'd been able to enjoy many leisurely hours with his family—something that, in the past, had been a luxury. For until February 1, 1961, he had been a career soldier, retiring as a lieutenant colonel after twenty-one years of continuous active duty which had taken him from the battlefields of Europe to the far outposts of the Orient.

A series of heart attacks precipitated his retirement on forty percent physical disability at the relatively youthful age of forty-six, when he still had a potential for many more years of useful service.

Since then, Whalen had worked only as a part-time $1.40-an-hour maintenance man during the summers with the Fairfax County Park Authority. It was an incongruous turn for a man who had been a high-ranking officer of the Army—most especially for one who had been discharging the delicate obligations of an intelligence officer and aide to the Joint Chiefs of Staff in the Pentagon.

But he had been unable to find anything with more prestige and better income. He had tried to capitalize on his years of experience as an intelligence officer by applying for a civilian position with the Defense Department. However, he had been turned down.

Outwardly, Whalen never betrayed discontent. He worked uncomplainingly, and his neighbors who had known him as a colonel, admired him for swallowing his pride.

Whalen had to work. He needed a supplementary income to meet payments on the twenty-five-thousand-dollar mortgage and other expenses of the comfortable thirty-eight-thousand-dollar split-level home he'd bought for his family. With his laborer's salary augmenting the five-thousand-dollar-a-year disability income from the Army, he managed to survive.

If this day of Tuesday, July 12, 1966, had been like other days, Whalen would have been at work at the park. And at four fifty-five P.M. when those six strangers came calling, he would have just been starting for home. But Whalen hadn't worked in more than three weeks, having been dismissed from his job on June 20.

There had been a dispute between him and his boss, Park Authority Director James D. Bell. It appears that Whalen had admitted taperecording a phone call from his wife to Bell on June 16. Whalen had claimed he taped the conversation because he wanted to know "what was going on in the parks."

In the call, Mrs. Whalen assertedly had complained that her husband was getting many phone calls at home on park business, and she had set up an appointment to see the director about it. However, she never showed up. The colonel's firing followed.

Thus it was on this late hot July afternoon that Whalen had spent the entire day at home, except for working with the shrubs and plants on his own grounds.

After his gardening chores Whalen went down to the den and

joined his daughter in front of the television to await Mrs. Whalen's call to supper. Father and daughter were so absorbed in the program that neither heard the doorbell chimes. But Mrs. Whalen promptly went to see who it was.

She was surprised but hardly startled to see the three tall strangers at her front door. Her first flash of thought was that they might be salesmen.

But automatically, another part of Mrs. Whalen's mind took in the other three men midway down the walk.

"Yes, gentlemen?" Mrs. Whalen said.

"We would like to see Colonel Whalen," said one of the men with a polite smile. "Is he at home? This is business."

The last words were spoken softly but conveyed a harsh, exacting note which instantly erased the idea from Mrs. Whalen's mind that these strangers might be salesmen. She asked the callers to wait at the door and went to summon her husband.

In seconds, Whalen had climbed the seven short steps from the den to the foyer and walked to the door. There was a somber expression on his face as he glanced at the three men. Vaguely he registered the presence of the other three strangers below on the walk.

"Colonel Whalen," said the man who'd spoken before, "may we come in and see you a moment—in private?"

Whalen looked at him blankly. "What is it you want to see me about?"

The man who had been doing the talking flipped open a small folded leather case in his right hand. Before Whalen's eyes could absorb the wording on the identification card, he heard "FBI."

Whalen took two steps backward. It was his invitation to the men to enter. He showed them into the living room and asked them to sit. But the FBI agents hadn't come to visit.

"I have a warrant, sir," the man who had been doing the talking said. "It was issued by the Federal Court in Newport News, and it is for your arrest on an indictment by the grand jury. The charges are espionage . . ."

Whalen's mouth dropped as he stared at the agents.

"Es-pionage?"

"That is right, sir," the G-man said politely. "Will you come along with us, please?"

The tall, lanky suspect whose short-cropped, graying brown hair and shoulders-back stance reflected the military man he'd been for nearly a quarter of a century, stood mute, his face the image of disbelief.

"If you want to change, Colonel . . ." the FBI man pressed him.

Whalen, who was dressed casually in gray work pants, blue and white striped sportshirt, and moccasins, shrugged his shoulders. He didn't care. He'd come along as he was. But first could he explain to his wife? It wouldn't be easy.

He was given permission to talk with Mrs. Whalen in the kitchen. Kitty was still in the den, her attention riveted on the TV program, unaware of the great drama suddenly enmeshing her father.

But was it suddenly? Or was this moment merely the culmination of a "conspiracy that began in the early part of 1959 and ran continuously into the early part of 1963," as the indictment handed up by the grand jury read?

The conspiracy was perhaps the most far-reaching, most damaging of any spy case in the nation's history, for it involved charges of selling the nation's top atomic and military secrets to the Russians over a four-year period. The heart of the indictment accused William H. Whalen of conspiring with two Soviet Embassy officials to supply data on a wide range of sensitive subjects:

"Information pertaining to atomic weaponry, missiles, military plans for the defense of Europe, estimates of comparative military capabilities, military intelligence reports and analysis, information concerning the retaliation plans by the United States Strategic Air

Command, and information pertaining to troop movements, documents, and writings relating to the national defense of the United States."

The good-byes between William and Bernadine were spoken softly. The parting brought tears to Mrs. Whalen's eyes.

As the G-men escorted the accused spy out the door, the scene from without to neighbors who might have been watching couldn't have commanded the faintest suspicion. These strangers who had approached so inconspicuously minutes before, might have been friends of the Colonel's who'd dropped by to have him join them on some excursion.

No one, in fact, would know that former Colonel William H. Whalen had been arrested for espionage until hours later, when the news broke sensationally.

Only the next morning did neighbors gather in small knots on the sidewalk or in clusters on the well-groomed lawns along Dewey Avenue, talking in subdued but shocked tones about "the Colonel's arrest."

By then, too, the neighborhood was overrun with reporters, photographers, and television newsmen, all looking eagerly for comment from the neighbors, after the initial assault upon the Whalen home for interviews had failed.

The news of Colonel Whalen's arrest as a Pentagon spy left many persons on the block stunned. Although few of the residents in the area seemed to know him well, all were aware of the man who'd worn the Army "pinks" with the lieutenant colonel's insignia on his shoulders and proudly sported the rows of colorful campaign ribbons on his breast.

One neighbor who lived across the street, had only words of praise for Whalen. "He was one of the kindest men in the neighborhood. Whenever anyone was in trouble he was the first one there," he said.

Another neighbor described himself as a friend of Whalen's and said he'd known him since long before his retirement. He remarked:

"I don't understand it. He was so patriotic. To his wife he was Army all the way. To all of us he was an outstanding gentleman and officer."

Still another neighbor spoke about the parties the Whalens had held at their house until the Colonel's retirement.

"They'd invite a lot of the people on the street to their affairs," the neighbor said. "They had some big Christmas parties. I remember meeting some persons at one of them in 1960, I believe, and I think they were introduced to me as Russians. But I didn't think that was unusual at the time because the Whalens had quite a few Embassy contacts."

One stunned housewife said:

"My God, this man was A-one all the way. I simply can't believe he could be a spy."

But one other woman on Dewey Avenue told a reporter that FBI men had made discreet inquiries in the neighborhood about the former Army officer two years before.

"I just didn't know what to think about it," she said, shaking her head. "I never suspected they were investigating him as a spy."

Reporters also reached Park Authority Director Bell, who revealed that the FBI had been to see him for information about Whalen. "They came the day after I dismissed him," Bell said. "They wanted to know why I had let him go."

After a long interlude, Mrs. Whalen finally opened the door to newsmen. She came out with red-rimmed eyes and trembling lips. For several seconds she faced the reporters wordlessly, then finally as a fresh flow of tears started down her cheeks she managed to speak in a choked, emotion-filled voice.

"It just isn't true, it just isn't true. He never said anything about this to me. Oh, what will I do now?"

Mrs. Whalen buried her head in her hands for a moment, then stared at the reporters.

"I never asked him questions about what he did. We've been married fourteen years and I knew him for seven years before that. I used to work for the Government, too, so I know what security is. That's why I never asked about what he was doing. I wasn't even allowed to go into his office when we were in Japan.

"I don't know how this could happen. It isn't possible. I don't believe it. I'll never believe it. What is going to become of our daughter?"

Mrs. Whalen paused to gather her thoughts.

"This can't be true," she started once more. "This is something that is so bad, the charges against my husband, that I know it can't be true. I'm so embarrassed. We'll never be able to live in this neighborhood again. . . . Who's going to pay the bills?"

Mrs. Whalen sighed in exasperation and stepped back into the house, closing the door. A little later, she left with a neighbor. Her face was pale and dark glasses hid her reddened eyes. She was on her way to Alexandria—for her husband's arraignment before U.S. Commissioner Alex Ackerman, Jr. in the U.S. Courthouse.

The shock and disbelief suddenly surrounding Colonel Whalen's arrest raised many questions about the conspiracy—its extent, duration, and its actual damage to the national security of the United States. But most of all it posed questions of how a military officer, thoroughly and meticulously screened for assignment with the Joint Chiefs of Staff could cross into the shadow world of espionage through that enormous and supposedly impenetrable wall of security that Uncle Sam had erected around the Pentagon.

The FBI knew precisely how it was done because, in its characteristically thorough way, it had catalogued the movements and background of the principal suspect, Whalen, almost from the beginning.

But even as the FBI was starting its surveillance, it began to examine virtually all of the important landmarks in William Whalen's life, to see if there was anything which might point to a capability to engage in something so heinous as espionage.

Whalen's early life provided no hint that he would someday enter either military life—or subversion.

William H. Whalen was born in 1916 in Watervliet, a suburb of Albany in upstate New York, the son of a locomotive engineer on the Delaware and Hudson Railroad. The family home at 718 Seventh Avenue was a stone's throw from a famed Civil War arsenal.

Here young William Whalen grew up with two brothers, John and Charles, and a sister, who has since died.

He attended St. Brigid's Elementary School, was graduated in 1927, then went to Catholic Central High School in nearby Troy, from which he was graduated in 1931. After that, he attended an embalmer's school, but never practiced the trade. In the late 1930's, he married a Troy girl, Virginia Hill. They took a place near his family home. Then he became interested in the New York National Guard and joined the unit headquartered in the old arsenal near his home.

Just before World War II he was injured in an auto accident in the Troy area which hospitalized him for several weeks and left his face severely scarred.

The year 1940 was important to Whalen in many ways. Early in the year, the gold bars of a second lieutenant in the National Guard were pinned on his shoulders, a commissioning ceremony which gave him officer-and-gentleman status in the military community.

The flames of war had already erupted in Europe, and the disaster of Pearl Harbor was not many months away when, on October 15, 1940, he began a full-time military career as his unit was federalized and transferred to duty at Fort McClellan, Alabama.

At Fort McClellan he became company commander in the 105th Infantry, then later served in that same capacity at Camp Forest, Tennessee.

In June, 1941, with war only six months away, he was transferred to Camp Stoneman, California, the sprawling port of embarkation in the San Francisco area where hundreds of thousands of Americans would ship out in the next few years to such exotic-sounding places as Guadalcanal, Zamboanga, Ulithi, Tarawa, Saipan, Guam, Okinawa, Iwo Jima, and Taipan.

Just as a soldier must be built up to a high peak of fighting tautness, he must also be provided a change of pace, chance to relax, to see a movie, to remember what things were like back in civilian life. This was the job of the Army's Special Services Forces, the unit engaged mainly in providing entertainment—both here at home military bases and in the battle zones of the Pacific and in Europe—such as programs of sports and recreation, and United Service Organization shows for the troops.

Being in Special Services was regarded by many of the fighting GI's as "soft duty," the greatest assignment in the world. And if you were a Special Services officer, they said, you "had it made"— who would want to leave the Army?

Lieutenant William H. Whalen found himself in this position in mid-1942. This was after he had been admitted to Letterman General Hospital at the Presidio, in San Francisco, in March of that year with an undisclosed illness. He was discharged in May and, after brief duty again as company commander with infantry troops, was transferred to the Special Services Forces.

For more than a year he provided recreation and talent in the bright sunshine of the American West. But the action was developing in Europe, where a vast armada was being assembled for the invasion.

In the bitter winter which began in December of 1943, William H. Whalen, now a captain, was assigned to the Special Services section of the Assembly Area Command of the European Theater's communications zone.

The invasion armada was launched by General Dwight D. Eisenhower the following June, and as the military divisions started to push the German legions back, the American fighting man had occasional opportunity to relax and Whalen was assigned to provide entertainment. He did the job so well that he was eventually transferred to the general staff of the continental base section in Europe in January, 1946. He became assistant secretary of the general staff, where he had more responsibility, more prestige, more importance. In June he became executive officer of the technical information branch of Special Services in the European Command. After a year, he was named chief of the branch, a job he held until December, 1947.

But now the war was over, and Whalen was eager to move into some other branch, something with more excitement, more significance, more challenge than Special Services. He was now a major.

Someone of high rank must have been watching his career and must have been impressed, for a jump from Special Services to the cloak-and-dagger world of the intelligence division—G-2—is certainly a major change. But that was Whalen's new assignment and it brought him back to the States with an assignment to the Army's general staff in the Pentagon.

Personal tragedy can change a man, upset his life, change his perspective, set up new patterns. William Whalen's marriage to Virginia Hill ended abruptly, but its termination has remained a mystery to those making a study of his background.

FBI men who trod the Watervliet-Albany-Troy area in search of information on Whalen were told that Virginia Hill had died. Yet, incongruously, other agents who dug into the records in Washington came up with evidence that William and Virginia had been divorced.

Whichever way it happened, William Whalen did not remain single very long. Washington, they say, is a city of five women for every man, and not unexpectedly, a young, now-available officer found himself another wife.

On March 17, 1952, according to the records of the city clerk in the nation's capital, William Henry Whalen, thirty-six, of Watervliet, N.Y., and Marjorie Elmore, thirty, of Memphis, Tennessee, applied for a marriage license. The records show further that Whalen and Miss Elmore were married at the Walter Reed Medical Center Chapel on April 12, 1952, by Army Chaplain Albert M. Schumacher, a Methodist clergyman.

On the marriage license application, the couple indicated that both were divorced. Whalen's first marriage assertedly ended in Alexandria, and Miss Elmore's in Memphis.

Inquiries in the capital also indicated that Whalen had been acquainted with Miss Elmore for some years prior to their marriage when she worked in a Government office.

Army records showed that almost immediately after the Whalens married, they left for Japan where he was sent to join the intelligence section of Army headquarters in Tokyo. Neither the marriage records nor the Army files on Whalen showed when or why his second wife changed her name from Marjorie to Bernadine. But it was Whalen, not his wife, who was the subject of the sweeping FBI study, which now turned its spotlight to his activities in the Orient.

Tokyo was rebuilding when Whalen arrived. The sprawling citadel of the Far East was turning into a modern outpost of the Western World.

From his office in the Dai Ichi Building he could look across a broad street and see the watery moat surrounding the Emperor's palace and Hibiya Park with its huge shrine and Hibiya Hall where the Nippon Symphony performed, incongruously, Bach, Beethoven, and Brahms.

In Japan, everyone collects something, and now Lieutenant Colonel William Whalen, proudly sporting the silver crest of his newly acquired rank, got the bug. He became an "antiquer," exploring the narrow, sometimes not so fragrant streets of Tokyo in search of bric-a-brac and animal figurines which captured his interest. One of his prized purchases was an ivory tiger carving which he claimed was worth seventy-eight hundred dollars. And he made the newspapers with picture and story when he offered to sell it for "five thousand dollars or more."

During his three-year tour of duty in Tokyo, Colonel Whalen also became something of a hero by persuading a Russian colonel in the Soviet Embassy there to defect to the American side.

In June, 1955, Whalen was returned to Washington and assigned to the Army's Assistant Chief of Staff, Intelligence Branch, for what was to be a two-year tour. And there were other joys to brighten the Colonel's outlook because now for the first time he had become a father. The birth of little Kitty also demanded roomier living quarters. The split-level on Dewey Drive in Fairfax County was the answer. And with only a small down payment plus a GI mortgage, the William Whalens now had a family home.

Meanwhile, the Colonel's career continued in the ascendancy as he was plucked from the Army's intelligence staff and assigned to the staff of the Joint Chiefs of Staff, the most sensitive and most responsible position any officer could hope to attain in the military. Now he was within the inner councils of America's highest military order. In time of war, it would be the men who sat behind those lofty desks in the Pentagon who would call the President on the "hot line" and advise him the time had come to unleash intercontinental ballistics missiles with atomic warheads upon the enemy.

Whalen's duties with the Joint Chiefs differed greatly from his work with Army Intelligence the previous two years when he had served on an inter-agency committee, based in the State Department, which makes plans for evacuation of American citizens from world trouble spots. Now he was dealing with such top-secret information as key atomic and missile weapons data, the military plans of the Strategic Air Command and its fighting strength and potential, the location and size of American—and Allied—military forces in Europe, and countless other vital aspects of our offensive and defensive military posture.

In its thoroughness, the FBI turned up all this historical data on Colonel William H. Whalen and brought them literally dovetailing with the very opening of its own on-the-spot surveillance of the officer who had all at once become the subject of investigation.

From early 1959 on, Colonel Whalen would never stray from the sight of an FBI agent—he would be watched constantly.

What action, what movement, what behavior on Colonel Whalen's part was it that precipitated the FBI inquiry into his conduct?

In fact, it was an accumulation of things. But nothing attracted more attention than Colonel Whalen's unexplained meetings with two Soviet Embassy officials, first observed by FBI agents in the early part of 1959. There was no clue as to why Whalen's non-working hours should be absorbed in contacts with either Colonel Sergei A. Edemski, the Assistant Military Attaché, or Mikhail M. Shumaev, the First Secretary of the Embassy. Nor was it clear why these secretive encounters were held in northern Virginia shopping centers.

To FBI men, Whalen's association with Edemski and Shumaev had the classic strains of an old familiar refrain—conspiracy. But the question still was: Could a man like Whalen, who didn't have to prove his patriotism to anyone because of long years of service to his country, be involved in anything so incredible as espionage?

Just meeting and talking with Soviet Embassy officials is not a crime. Couldn't Whalen be meeting and talking with Edemski and Shumaev about defecting—as he had with the Soviet colonel in Japan?

But whatever the answer, the FBI had decided too much was at stake to waste time with idle speculation. Whalen not only had to be watched constantly, but his superiors on the Joint Chiefs of Staff would have to be alerted.

However, there was a problem the FBI had never encountered

before. In all other cases that had come to the Bureau's attention, all that had to be done was to cut off the flow of actual information by "planting" false and misleading data, giving the Government time to determine the full nature and scope of the operation and learn the identity of everyone involved in the plot.

But how do the Joint Chiefs of Staff play games with the nation's super-secrets?

At this level there is no place to conceal information, no room to plant doctored reports—no one with the slightest taint of suspicion can be tolerated. He must be removed immediately because the peril is too great. Yet if a man like Whalen were a spy, might it not be conceivable that others—even higher ranking officers—could be involved?

It became necessary to alert military counterintelligence agents about the FBI investigation. This was done at the very highest level; even President Eisenhower was consulted.

The decision: Let Whalen stay where he is—and watch him.

The G-men never actually witnessed an overt act of espionage during their early observations of Whalen's meetings with the Russians, which occurred with most frequency at the Telegraph Road Shopping Center, at Telegraph Road and Farmington Drive in Alexandria—directly across the street from Jefferson Manor Park (where one day in the future Whalen would work as grounds keeper).

But sometime in May, 1959, the G-men spotted Colonel Whalen meeting furtively at that shopping center with Sergei Edemski and Mikhail Shumaev, who was also known by the code name of "Mike," and observed the Russians handing the American an envelope. According to the FBI, there was a thousand dollars in that envelope for Whalen.

There was no indication of what specific information Whalen turned over at this or subsequent meetings, but the FBI said the Colonel's method was to note down classified data that came his way in the Pentagon, and to encourage other officers to tell him about their activities.

In the months ahead, other payments were assertedly made in the same manner, at this and other shopping centers in Arlington County. Now, however, the meetings were only with Shumaev, because Edemski had been relieved of his duties and sent back to Moscow.

Then came November, 1960, and Whalen was suddenly confined to DeWitt Hospital at Fort Belvoir, Virginia, the Army Engineers Corps' big base fifteen miles south of the Pentagon. He had suffered a heart attack.

He remained a patient for two months, but during his confinement, in December, 1960, he apparently was well enough to make his way out of the hospital and take a five-hundred-dollar payment from the Russians at a shopping center in Alexandria.

Discharged from DeWitt, Whalen returned to his office in the Pentagon in February, 1961, only to find he had been relieved of active duty and placed on the temporarily disabled retired list. But his meetings with "Mike" continued and he was spotted with the Russian once again in March at an Alexandria shopping center. The FBI said the Soviet Embassy First Secretary paid Whalen one thousand dollars at this meeting for more information. So far, the FBI computed that Whalen had received fifty-five hundred dollars.

After this, with Whalen out of the service, the meetings with Shumaev became less frequent—and the payments stopped.

Yet Whalen didn't stop trying to get back into the Pentagon. In October, 1962, after some prodding by "Mike," Whalen applied for a civilian job in intelligence, but was turned down. After that he met "Mike" only occasionally. His usefulness to the Russians apparently had come to an end. And so, too, had "Mike's" usefulness. In September, 1963, Mikail M. Shumaev was recalled to Moscow.

The Government didn't indicate whether Whalen was involved

in any further conspiracy after this, nor did it say at his arraignment before U.S. Commissioner Ackerman why it took until July 12, 1966, to finally bring action against the former Colonel.

Whalen was handcuffed as he was brought into court and seemed downcast and confused when questions were put to him by the court. U.S. Attorney C. Vernon Spratley, Jr., who not long before had closed out the Johnson-Mintkenbaugh case, put in no objection to the fifteen-thousand-dollar bail ordered by the court "because of Whalen's severe heart condition."

Mrs. Whalen raised the bond quickly by putting up the nineteen thousand dollars equity in their home as security for the fifteen thousand dollars, and Whalen was released for a later hearing when a trial date was set on the Federal Court calendar in Alexandria for December 19 before Judge Oren R. Lewis.

Even as preparations were being made for the trial, many of the unanswered—and half-answered—questions became a part of the intrigue triggered by William Whalen's arrest. The State Department admitted that Whalen had had limited access to "non-secret information during the two years he served on the interagency committee, from 1955 to 1957," but no one could explain how plans for the evacuation of American citizens from world trouble spots had so suddenly become "non-secret."

Although the indictment spoke in terms of the conspirators' intent, it didn't say how much information Colonel Whalen passed along. The Defense Department would only say that it first learned of the "security problem" many months ago.

"The facts," said the Pentagon, "were given special attention in our continuing effort to effect improvements in security, particularly as regards security trustworthiness of personnel in sensitive positions, and adequacy of control over the handling of classified documents."

But from other Pentagon sources, word came that when the Joint Chiefs of Staff learned about the nature of the compromised evidence, particularly their war plans, feverish and wholesale revisions and changes were rushed through to repair the damage.

No one part of the compromised data could be called of deeper significance to national security than the other—all were considered the most vital American military secrets in existence.

On Friday, December 16, three days before the trial was to begin, William Henry Whalen appeared unexpectedly before Judge Lewis for a hearing requested by the Justice Department. Earlier there had been reports that Whalen and his lawyer had visited the U.S. Attorney's office in Alexandria.

Even before the proceeding got under way, the outcome was predictable. Veteran reporters who had covered other espionage cases, the most recent involving former Airman Robert Glenn Thompson and Johnson-Mintkenbaugh, found it easy to guess why the government and Whalen were in court.

Whalen was asked by Judge Lewis if he understood what the hearing was all about and if he had any objection to the Government's new representation of charges against him. Whalen said he had no objections.

The Government had decided to drop the espionage charge which carried life imprisonment upon conviction.

Once more, following the precedent of cases involving the other Americans accused of espionage, the Government apparently had found it could not prosecute successfully for lack of a solid case. The two co-conspirators, Edemski and Shumaev, were immune from prosecution because of their diplomatic status. And they were not available as witnesses because they were out of the country.

What evidence had been mustered against Whalen was, for the most part, circumstantial. If the case went to trial, the prosecution might not be able to convince the jury of Whalen's guilt in espionage or, for that matter, of his guilt of the other charges—conspiring with Soviet agents to obtain documents connected with the national defense and conspiring with Soviet agents to act as a representative of the Soviet Union without registering with the Secretary of State.

And if the Government obtained a conviction on one or more of the charges, there was always the possibility that the verdict might be upset by the U.S. Supreme Court. In recent times the high court has tended more and more to overturn verdicts obtained with the mere testimony of Federal agents and statements or confessions submitted as evidence of a defendant's guilt. The court has taken the position that unless counsel is present when such statements or confessions are made, the defendant's Constitutional rights have been violated.

The author has learned that Whalen had made statements to the FBI and they were to have been submitted as evidence at his trial —but the prosecution was not prepared to show that the accused man had made those statements in his lawyer's presence. It was a virtual certainty that the statements would not pass the court's muster and would have been suppressed.

The proceeding in court was very brief. The two remaining charges were read to Whalen. How did he wish to plead, Judge Lewis asked?

"Guilty, your Honor," replied the defendant in a quiet, somber voice.

Judge Lewis immediately revoked Whalen's fifteen-thousand-dollar bond and ordered him held in the custody of the United States marshal until a probation report was submitted to the court. Whalen was handcuffed and escorted to the detention pen.

On March 2, 1967, Judge Lewis passed sentence on Whalen, giving him ten years on the conspiracy charge and five for failing to register as a foreign agent. The terms were to be served consecutively, which meant a total of fifteen years in Federal prison for Whalen.

Even after Whalen was sentenced, the Government made no effort to shed further light on the details of the case or to explain officially what data he transmitted to the Russians. The official silence promped the *Washington Post* to ask:

"Did the Defense Department or its intelligence arm, the Defense Intelligence Agency, shun arrests earlier to avoid a public disclosure of sensitive leaked information until it became obsolete?

"Was the Cold War, which was at its coldest in the 1959 to 1961 period of the alleged conspiracy, a factor in the timing of the arrest?

"Did any vital information actually change hands?

"If it did, how could a leak occur in the Pentagon's inner sanctum of officers, who are chosen for their loyalty and ability?"

No reply to these questions came from any official Government source—nor, for that matter, from the Russians. But the other side wasn't completely silent in response to the charges that Edemski and Shumaev were Whalen's co-conspirators.

From London, where Sergei A. Edemski was stationed with the Soviet Embassy, came this comment:

"Yes, I know Colonel Whalen . . . but I'm no spy or contact man."

Shumaev, incidentally, was no longer a colonel. He had been promoted to major general. After all, he had been instrumental in doing what no Russian spy had succeeded in doing in all the years that the Kremlin has been reconnoitering in the United States.

He penetrated the Pentagon—right up to the Joint Chiefs of Staff. How much higher can one go?

12

Red Satellite Spies Join the Act: Try to Bug the U.S. State Department

"Vzdysky ne velmi tesi kbyz Zas vidimi," greeted the smiling official seated behind the spacious, mahogany desk inside the severe-looking gray stone building of the Czechoslovakian diplomatic corps in Washington.

Frank John Mrkva nodded at this salutation which meant simply, "It is always a pleasure to see you, my friend."

This was a typical welcome each time he entered the Czech Embassy on Massachusetts Avenue. But what followed on this particular afternoon was new in Mrkva's experience.

"I have been meaning to ask you for a long time to come to one of our Embassy parties," the Czech emissary said. "Why don't you and Mrs. Mrkva come tomorrow night as my guests? You will enjoy yourselves tremendously and it will be an opportunity to meet some very fine people."

Mrkva stood stiffly in front of the desk trying not to betray the suspicion he felt at the surprising invitation. He let a thin smile crease his slender, elongated face.

"Thank you for asking me," he said. "And I know Mrs. Mrkva will be delighted. We shall be here . . . at eight o'clock tomorrow night, did you say?"

"Yes," beamed the man behind the desk, rising to shake hands with Mrkva.

As he stepped out of the Embassy into the street, Mrkva turned up his coat collar against a chilling wind sweeping along Massachusetts Avenue. A thickening mist was settling on Washington, limiting visibility to a few hundred feet and obscuring the Capitol's lofty dome. It made Mrkva feel he was being enveloped by a strange shroud that for a lack of logic spelled s-u-b-v-e-r-s-i-o-n.

Why should John Mrkva feel the invitation from Zdenek Pisk, the Czech Embassy's Second Secretary, might be an overture to villainy?

Perhaps because Frank John Mrkva was a diplomatic courier for the U.S. State Department and because he'd been alerted about approaches that might be made to him on his rounds, particularly invitations and solicitations by Iron Curtain diplomats.

The Czech Embassy was just one stop on Mrkva's daily rounds; his duties would take him to many other missions.

Now, there are couriers and there are couriers. Some deliver routine papers and documents; others carry briefcases full of dull facts and figures.

Not Mrkva. In his travels from his office on Pennsylvania Avenue to the Czechoslovakian Embassy a half mile away on Massachusetts, he would very often carry official papers which could open America's doors to anyone the Czechs wanted to bring into this country.

The lanky, dark-complexioned thirty-eight-old American-born Frank John Mrkva, son of immigrant parents from Czechoslovakia, was eminently qualified for his courier assignment because he spoke flawless Czech; that gave him the advantage of understanding exactly what the boys in the Czech Embassy were saying when visa applications were wanted—and of being understood himself by them.

In dealing with Mrkva, the diplomats from Prague apparently came to believe that anyone with such important documents as State Department passports must be highly placed—and should be able to get into many of the most secret places of the United States Government.

In retrospect then, it shouldn't seem too surprising that Mrkva eventually received the invitation to the Czech Embassy party that day back in the late winter of 1961, a day which stamped his entry into the world of spies and counterspies just as indelibly as the official seal impressed upon American passports he carried in his attaché case.

But the motivation was barely perceptible at first and even Mrkva had no reason to see a ploy behind the solicitation—except that he had been well briefed in advance to be wary of such overtures from Communist bloc countries. His orders were to report them immediately to his superiors.

Mrkva, born in Beaver Falls, Pennsylvania, and an Army veteran of the Korean War, had worked for nearly six years in the passport division—he first went into Government service with the State Department in 1955—without experiencing a single suspicious encounter with Czechs, Russians, or any other Communist representative on his rounds of their embassies.

He had found the persons he dealt with friendly, sociable, and interesting. They bore no resemblance to the classic spies of fiction that he'd read about, or the real-life ones that he'd been warned to beware.

Toward the end of 1960 and early in 1961, however, he began to detect an increased cordiality from certain Czech Embassy officials.

The change was so subtle at first that it didn't occur to Mrkva that he was being wooed—until that afternoon of March 14, 1961, when he made a routine trip to the Czech Embassy.

And now as he walked to the curb and got into the State Department sedan he'd parked in front of the Embassy, he wondered with rising concern about the invitation. It gnawed at him increasingly as he coursed through the rapidly thickening evening rush-hour traffic toward his office.

The invitation was all the more puzzling since it had come not from just an ordinary Embassy attaché, but from ranking Second Secretary Zdenek Pisk.

Why, Mrkva asked himself, should this man invite me—a mere courier—to be his guest at an Embassy function?

In his office, Mrkva opened his attaché case, removed the passport applications the Czechs had submitted for approval, and dropped them into a hopper that would take them through channels for processing.

Then he walked down a long corridor of opaque glass-paneled walls that concealed the army of clerks, stenographers, typists, and lower echelon supervisors in the passport division, and entered the office of the chief counsel of the passport office, Robert D. Johnson.

Mrkva was uneasy about how readily he had acquiesced to the dinner invitation.

He wasn't certain how his superior would react. But Mrkva found Johnson pleased at being advised about the unusual encounter with the Second Secretary.

"Well, now," Johnson said, "I believe this is important enough to take up with the powers-that-be. It may turn out to be nothing, then again—you never can tell what may happen."

Johnson phoned the director of the passport division, quickly touching off a chain of other hasty calls to higher echelons that finally reached the office of Undersecretary of State George W. Ball.

By now it had been agreed at all levels that the FBI must be advised immediately about the dinner bid to Mrkva; agents were sent over within the hour for an interview with the courier. Mrkva told them every detail.

Then, for the better part of that evening, the courier was briefed by the G-men on precisely how to conduct himself in the presence of the Czech Embassy crowd. And most important—to be wary of any requests, however innocent-sounding.

"They may not ask you for a single solitary thing," Mrkva was advised. "You may leave the party wondering why they invited you. But possibly the next day, a week later, or months afterward you may be asked to do something for them. Whenever that time comes you must be alert to recognize the approach and report it at once."

Mrkva listened closely to the advice of the FBI agents. In a way, he was beginning to feel he was the central figure in a potentially explosive spy drama, and yet he had no apparent grounds for harboring that notion. After all, an invitation to him and his wife to a diplomatic dinner, even from a Red satellite envoy like Zdenek Pisk, wasn't necessarily an overture to villainy.

Couldn't Pisk have simply taken a fancy to Mrkva for what he was—a dedicated, conscientious, sociable diplomatic courier, performing a valuable function for his own country that was proving worthwhile to the Czechs? Why couldn't this merely be the Czechs' way of showing appreciation?

Mrkva went home late that evening to his waiting wife, whom he'd phoned earlier and told he'd be delayed. He didn't mention his long session with the FBI, nor did he say anything about it when he reached home.

But he broke the news of the invitation to the Czech Embassy party, as he was supposed to, and expressed pleasure that this honor was tendered. His wife was equally pleased.

The party was an amalgam of excited laughter and chatter, and Mrkva and his wife found that their enjoyment of the evening's festivities was heightened greatly by Second Secretary Pisk's exuberant and concentrated attention on them. He introduced the State Department courier and his wife to every couple he could corner.

But through all the ceremony that began with hors d'oeuvres and drinks and ended with a formal state dinner and dancing, Mrkva never once was given the slightest hint that he was there for any other purpose but good fellowship.

The evening ended in a series of warm farewells as dignitaries from the Czech Mission said their good nights to Mrkva and his wife.

"You must come back again, you wonderful people," Pisk beamed as he escorted the couple to the door. "I shall see to it that you are our guests again at one of our functions."

Mrkva and his wife talked animatedly on their way home, recounting the highlights of the evening that had pleased them both immensely. He never let on that he'd gone to the Embassy in the cloak of a double-agent, and Mrs. Mrkva had no good reason to suspect her husband was anything more than what he'd always been—a State Department courier.

The next morning, Mrkva was interviewed privately by FBI agents in Johnson's office. He gave them a full rundown on the party.

"It isn't much," said one of the G-men. "But that shouldn't fool us. Let's keep our antennas up. They may make their approach another way, another time."

Mrkva continued his trips to the Czech Embassy as routinely as always. He failed to detect even the hint of an effort by Secretary Pisk to cultivate a friendship which exceeded the bounds already reached. The Czech diplomat remained cordial and convivial.

Spring and summer passed without a single new development and it began to appear that the invitation to the Embassy party that night was simply something that had to be accepted at face value.

But then came fall—and another invitation. Again Mrkva

accepted and again he took his wife. And once more nothing extraordinary happened.

As the end of November approached, it began to seem that the Czechs were not, after all, on a fishing expedition.

Then came November 30, a day that began like most other days for Mrkva as he sauntered into the Czech Embassy on another routine mission. After greeting Mrkva, Secretary Pisk unexpectedly approached the courier and said, "John, my friend, what do you say about having dinner with me tonight?"

"Do you mean another Embassy party?" Mrkva asked.

"No, I mean a private dinner—just you and I. There is something I want to discuss with you."

Mrkva smiled, "I will be delighted."

Pisk named a restaurant in the heart of the capital.

"Meet me there at seven-thirty," he said firmly, offering no further explanation.

On his return to the State Department, Mrkva promptly went to the office of the passport division's chief counsel and told him about the dinner engagement. Bob Johnson immediately summoned the FBI agents who had been on the case.

"This sounds like the opening they've been working up to," one of the G-men said. He instructed Mrkva to keep the date, then went over old ground on how to conduct himself in the Czech diplomat's presence. In the event of a proposition, Mrkva was told, accept it. But play it cool. Don't get too deeply involved. Let the FBI guide you.

At home that evening as he prepared for his dinner engagement, Mrkva told his wife of the appointment but offered the explanation that the office had assigned him on official business. Which was the truth—as far as it went.

Because Mrs. Mrkva was not a prober or the type to ply her husband with questions, he wasn't compelled to fabricate details.

The dinner with Pisk was casual and unhurried. It was also

somewhat of a mystery to Mrkva. The two men had sat, talking and eating, for an hour or more without the reason for the meeting becoming apparent. Mrkva wondered whether Pisk wasn't just trying to be friendly again.

Not until the waiter brought their after-dinner cordials did Mrkva detect the first faint ticking of some hidden works in the invitation. It began with a few random questions about Mrkva's family background and discreet inquiries about relatives in Czechoslovakia.

Then Pisk asked about Mrkva's duties at the State Department. The queries were innocuous and indirect at first. Gradually, however, they began to home in on specific areas.

Mrkva had no difficulty fielding the general questions. But when they became pointed and probing he had to fight a growing uneasiness which he tried to conceal with a contrived casual air.

He was a good actor. Mrkva managed to maintain his composure even though he had stiffened inwardly at the growing inquisitiveness of his host, who was now asking about State Department officials, their room numbers, about the director of the Office of Eastern European Affairs, the layout of his conference room, and other information.

But the most disconcerting sequence came when Pisk bluntly turned to Mrkva's own private affairs and cast a searchlight on his personal finances and problems.

Incredibly, the Czech emissary knew almost everything there was to know about Mrkva's economic balance sheet. He knew about the mortgage he owed on his house and about various debits and credits on his household ledger.

Then even more incredibly, he revealed that he knew about Mrkva's young daughter needing an operation.

"You can use some help, I see," Pisk said bluntly. "I believe that I may be able to help . . . to do something for you."

Mrkva looked aghast. He was supposed to. He had been coached by the FBI agents to exhibit surprise if Pisk—or any other official from the Czech Embassy—made a money offer.

"What I want to find out," Pisk said slowly, "is how passports are issued and what security measures are taken to protect them."

Mrkva knew this information was classified. He also was cognizant of the FBI's admonition not to release any information unless it had been cleared by the Bureau. He'd been told that if he was put on a spot, to give them the old "stall."

"I don't have that information at my fingertips," he half-whispered to Pisk. "But I'm confident I can get it for you. All I need is just a little time."

Pisk seemed pleased. He asked Mrkva to get the answers as soon as he could and to drop them off to him on one of his courier rounds.

"You don't have to be afraid of anything," Pisk lent his assurance gratuitously to the man he was trying to lead into subversion. "We shall take good care of you and your family. That is the truth."

Pisk paid the check, tipped the waiter, and walked with Mrkva to the door. They shook hands, then went their separate ways.

In the morning, Mrkva huddled with the FBI agents again in Johnson's office and related everything about his dinner meeting with the Czech delegate.

The FBI quickly gathered the information Pisk had requested and gave it to Mrkva for transmittal. Of course it was prepared with the assistance of State Department personnel—and carefully doctored.

Mrkva delivered the data to Pisk at the Czech Embassy on the afternoon of December 4. As he placed it in Pisk's hands, the Third Secretary took an envelope out of his pocket and gave it to the courier.

"This is a token of our appreciation," smiled Pisk. "And there is more where this came from. Much more."

Mrkva didn't open the envelope. He merely stuffed it into his pocket and brought it back to the State Department where he turned it over still sealed to Johnson and the G-men. When they tore the flap off they found ten crisp ten-dollar bills.

"Not a bad start," quipped Johnson.

The cash was impounded by the FBI, as are all such payoffs to double-agents. The role of the counterspy in Uncle Sam's employ is strictly a nonprofit venture. The only dividend the individual derives comes from the satisfaction that he has done a patriotic deed for his country.

And that's the way Frank John Mrkva felt as he pursued his assignment in counterespionage, heading toward an uncertain future. He had no idea where it would lead, nor how long it might last. But wherever it took him, however long it might be, he was willing to do it.

Not more than a fortnight after his first encounter with Pisk in the restaurant, Mrkva was invited out to dinner again. And once more Pisk wanted information—this time telephone book data.

"I want the extensions of all the top officials in the State Department," the Czech diplomat demanded boldly.

As before, the FBI cleared the list and Mrkva put it in Pisk's hands in exchange for another envelope bearing a hundred-dollar gratuity.

It went like that through January into February, then March and April. By May, Mrkva had had nearly a dozen meetings with Pisk. Their rendezvous were not always in restaurants. Sometimes they met on park benches in the capital or across the Potomac in Arlington; there were occasional get-togethers in supermarket parking lots; and they also met in front of several theaters. Once they even met outside the gates of the White House!

Then came May 8, 1963, when Mrkva met Pisk again for dinner. It came as a complete surprise to the courier when the Czech diplomat advised him of "an important change that will take place."

"They are recalling me to Prague for other duties," Pisk told Mrkva. "But that doesn't bring your important work to an end. It is only the beginning of a new phase. From now on you will deal with a friend of mine. He will guide you and tell you what we want done."

The friend, Pisk told Mrkva, was Jiri Opatrny, an Embassy attaché. The mention of the name prompted the courier to burst into laughter. Mrkva, who knew Czech fluently, translated the name into English and it came out "George Careful."

When he began to deal with Opatrny, Mrkva found a different personality. Jiri, or George as Mrkva often called him, had none of Pisk's subtlety and suaveness.

"With George, it seems to me," Mrkva told the FBI after one of his early meetings with him, "it's a question of what George wants. He's not like Pisk. He's more open. He puts everything on the line."

George first tried political indoctrination by espousing the merits of Communist governments. But Mrkva didn't bite. So George tried talking dollars and cents and soon found that he had an avid listener. Also a very surprised one.

Opatrny seemed to know a great deal more about Mrkva's finances than Pisk. He also appeared to have authority to spend more for information.

"Please keep in mind that I am prepared to pay for your daughter's operation," Opatrny informed Mrkva. Then he added, "And I would also like to help you along with your mortgage payments." George told Mrkva he couldn't understand how anyone could keep up with the installments on a thirty-year mortgage such as the State Department courier was carrying.

"He must have run a thorough credit check on me," Mrkva finally told the FBI. "He knows who I owe and how much I owe better than I do."

For the next three years—until May, 1966—Mrkva continued to provide Opatrny with the data he requested. But always after

State Department officials and the FBI had cleared it. Never did Mrkva undertake on his own to supply any data.

During those thirty-six months Mrkva filled such requests as a blank U.S. passport of a new series, information on the layout of rooms occupied by department officers dealing with Czechoslovakia, but most particularly information about the offices of the director of the Office of Eastern European Affairs, and the conference room he used.

When Mrkva relayed this last request back to his superiors and the FBI, no one could quite figure out why George wanted that information. It was just as puzzling when Mrkva was asked to obtain a General Services Administration catalog of Government furniture.

But gradually the mystery began to clear. "George Careful's" objective in obtaining the catalog was to learn from Mrkva precisely what style of furniture was used to furnish the office of OEEA Director Raymond Lisle. Not until May 29 did Mrkva, his superiors, and the FBI become aware of what value the catalog was to Opatrny and the Czechs.

On that day Opatrny delivered into Mrkva's hands a small rectangular wooden case whose dimensions were thirteen inches in length, one and one-quarter inches in width, and a half-inch in thickness.

It had been handcarved in the same design and craftsmanship, and stained in the same mahogany tone as the furniture in Lisle's office. It might have seemed harmless enough if it weren't for an aperture that made it a dead giveaway.

The case concealed a powerful miniature radio transmitter which could be turned on and off by remote control with an electronic signal!

"You are to place this in Mr. Lisle's office," Opatrny directed. Mrkva had given espionage agents credit for ingenuity, but this exceeded anything he imagined might be attempted against a privileged sanctuary such as the United States State Department in Washington.

Opatrny instructed Mrkva in its exact placement. "It goes under the bookcase. It was made to fit right here . . ."

The Czech Embassy attaché pointed to the General Services catalog photo of the bookcase in Lisle's office. "And," Opatrny offered with a smile, "there is going to be one thousand dollars for you in the next envelope when you have completed this little chore."

Mrkva went back to the State Department and put the transmitter into the FBI's hands. Lisle was called into a strategy session.

"We'll go along with the ploy," the OEEA director said.

The device was placed precisely where Opatrny said it should be and the FBI went so far as to "cooperate" with the Communists by allowing the transmitter to send out twenty minutes of harmless conversation. Then it was turned off, taken out—and taken apart.

Examination showed that the wooden case and the tiny radio receiver-transmitter apparently were made in Czechoslovakia—but there was one "Made in the U.S.A." touch. Power for the device was supplied by seven American-manufactured dry-cell batteries!

For security reasons the range capability of the transmitter was never to be revealed, the authorities agreed. But presumably it was powerful enough to send out its very high-frequency radio signals to the Czech Embassy on Massachusetts Avenue, a half-mile north of the State Department Building.

Mrkva didn't see Opatrny again until a week later. The Czech attaché greeted his agent with mixed emotions.

"I don't understand it," Opatrny complained. "The listening device worked beautifully after you installed it. But then it suddenly stopped. Have you any idea why?"

Mrkva fell into deep thought for a moment. "I wonder," he mused, "if what I did had anything to do with that . . ."

"What did you do!" demanded "Careful George."

Mrkva scratched his head, gazed deep into Opatrny's eyes, and sighed, "I dropped it."

"Then that is what is wrong with it," Opatrny shot back. "Go there and take it out. Bring it to me. I will get it repaired."

That was all right with Mrkva, except for one thing.

"You haven't paid me anything yet. After all, I am taking some awful chances."

"All right, all right," Opatrny said curtly. He dug his hand into the inside of his jacket and withdrew an envelope.

"Here, there is five hundred dollars in the envelope."

"But you promised me one thousand—"

"Yes, when you have completed the job and the transmitter is working. Now go get it and bring it to me so I can get it fixed."

Mrkva promised to do his best to get it back, but said he didn't know when he'd have an opportunity to get into Lisle's office unobserved.

"You must try," Opatrny said in parting.

Two days later, on June 9, 1966, Mrkva met the Czech delegate again.

"I have bad news," the counterspy said thinly. "I haven't been able to get at that device yet. I've had no opportunity to go up to Mr. Lisle's office. There's going to have to be a delay."

Opatrny was infuriated. "I think you are giving me the business, I don't believe you ever installed the transmitter in Lisle's office."

An argument ensued. It ended in a standoff. The two men met on several more occasions and there were more heated discussions. What it all boiled down to was that Mrkva wasn't going to return the transmitter because Opatrny showed "bad faith."

And there stood the case—transmitter and all—in a state of limbo for the next thirty days. Then in late June, 1966, Opatrny sent Mrkva a message to the State Department (by now Mrkva had been promoted from courier to a position in the passport division offices). Opatrny wanted to get together with Mrkva.

On the advice of his superiors and the FBI, Mrkva met "Careful George," who was all smiles once again.

"You know, John," Opatrny said in a voice dripping with sweetness, "we should continue to work closely together. There is so much that remains to be done."

"What are your plans?" Mrkva asked.

"There are other offices besides Lisle's that we want to place listening devices."

"Which ones?"

"Oh, there is . . . Undersecretary Ball's office is one . . ."

"Do you really want Mr. Ball's office bugged?" asked Mrkva with a straight face.

"Yes, yes . . . but before we do anything else everyone wants to know what is wrong with the listening device you placed in Lisle's office. Do you think . . . can you get it back?"

Mrkva shook his head. "No, my friend, you didn't hold up your end of the bargain. I'm sorry . . ."

Mrkva turned and walked away—exactly as he'd been told to do by the FBI.

Exactly one week later, on Wednesday, July 14—just twenty-four hours after the revelation that Colonel William Henry Whalen had been arrested as a Pentagon spy—the State Department made public the entire Czech spy plot to the nation. At the same time the department told the Czech Embassy that Jiri Opatrny had been declared persona non grata and was ordering him to leave the country within three days.

As for Zdenek Pisk, who had left the country in 1963, he was back in the United States, serving as First Secretary of the Czech Mission to the United Nations. But although the State Department advised Secretary General U Thant about Pisk's "previous activities," there was nothing that could be done to oust him from his post in New York.

A technicality saved him. Pisk didn't become a delegate until May 30, when he returned to this country from Prague, while the

State Department account indicated the case had been resolved before that.

But Opatrny had no defense and had to depart for his native Czechoslovakia. He went back, the State Department and FBI said, minus his miniature radio receiver-transmitter.

As for Frank John Mrkva, he was a hero all the way. He was rewarded with a promotion from the civil service grade of GS-11 to GS-12, a two-thousand-dollar-a-year salary increase—and was toasted coast to coast on radio and TV programs, interviewed by newspapers and magazines, and even presented with an honor award by the State Department.

Mrkva helped prove once again that the Communists are creatures of habit when it comes to espionage. The FBI's alertness has frustrated their efforts time and time again—but they always try again.

It was the first known attempt by a foreign power to place a listening device in a Government installation in this country, but not the first elsewhere. There have been numerous Communist attempts—some successful—in placing eavesdropping equipment in American embassies in the Soviet Union and other Communist countries. The classic case was the one in which the Russians secreted a "bug" in the beak of the American eagle at the Embassy in Moscow—and Henry Cabot Lodge, the former American Ambassador to the United Nations, demonstrated the evidence before a packed, and startled, session of the General Assembly.

But the Czech scheme was the first known attempt to bug the U.S. State Department—and thanks to Frank John Mrkva, a patriotic American, the plot failed.

13

Our Surveyor on the Moon—a Prize
for Red Spies

The distance between the moon's barren Ocean of Storms and the headquarters of the American Association of University Women in Washington, D. C., is roughly 231,400 miles. And when America's Surveyor I made its historic landing on the flat lunar landscape on June 2, 1966, and began transmitting television pictures from the face of the celestial body to living room television sets, this most sophisticated electronic marvel brought ringing praise from around the world—even grudging kudos from the project's keenest observers, the Russians.

Soviet space scientists were highly impressed by the success in maneuvering the 220-pound Surveyor I into the soft-landing on the lunar crust. But Tass took pains to remind the Russian people that this triumph of space technology by the United States had been preceded by the landing of Lunar 9 on the moon four months before, on February 3, 1966.

"The photographs and information transmitted by the Soviet moon station," boasted Tass, "helped the Americans to overcome quickly the difficulties involved . . ."

What the Soviet news agency failed to mention were the difficulties that Russia's own scientists developing the Luna probe had encountered—and how their problems may have been overcome by information transmitted by the Third Secretary of the Soviet Embassy in Washington.

There was no mention of Valentin A. Revin, a dark, brooding, gentle-faced man of scientific background. Nor was anything said about the headquarters of the American Association of University Women in Washington.

It was at these headquarters in the spring of 1961 that Valentin Revin made his initial quest for information and material relating to the Surveyor project, which had been conceived a year earlier by the National Aeronautics and Space Administration.

No secrecy was attached to the fact that NASA had begun development of a spacecraft intended to land scientific instruments and cameras on the moon for exploration of its surface. Many stories about the project had been published in newspapers and magazines. Even sketches and drawings of the proposed vehicle had been released to the public.

Moreover the names of the firms that would produce the various components, from the giant Atlas-Centaur rocket that was to boost the Surveyor beyond earth's gravity to the smaller liquid-fueled jets for cushioning the craft's fall upon the moon's landscape, and its scientific instruments and cameras as well, were all revealed in accounts about the program.

So it was no great surprise that an enterprising Soviet agent-diplomat with a background in science like Valentin Revin sought out an American like John Huminik at the technical meeting in the auditorium of the American Association of University Women.

Huminik, slender, dark-haired, bespectacled, was a man to

know. At twenty-six, he was already a partner and vice-president of the Value Engineering Company, headquartered across the Potomac in Alexandria. Among Value's scientific endeavors were projects in missile and space development. More important, Huminik was rapidly developing some prominence in the area of lunar exploration and study because of special work he was doing in that field.

Third Secretary Revin may or may not have known about John Huminik when he walked into the meeting that afternoon as casually as though he were one of the invited engineers. Revin's ticket of admission was his gall. He simply strolled up to the reception desk in the lobby, apologized for losing his invitation, and was allowed in. Revin had never been invited.

Once inside, the Russian quickly gravitated toward Huminik, who happened to be looking toward the door when Revin entered.

"Hello," the Soviet diplomat said with a smile. "I am Valentin Revin, a member of the scientific staff at the Soviet Embassy."

Huminik coughed to clear his throat at this unexpected encounter.

"How do you do," he said after a moment, shaking hands. "My name is John Huminik."

"That is not an Irish name?" the Soviet diplomat asked jocularly.

"Hardly," the engineer laughed politely. "As a matter of fact it happens to be Russian."

"Then we have something very important in common," Revin said pleased. He put his head back and glanced at Huminik as if trying to analyze him.

"With what firm are you connected?" the man from the Embassy asked. He acted surprised when Huminik told him of his connection with Value Engineering.

"You must be a genius," Revin said quickly. "Why you are so young—and already an executive. I cannot believe it."

Revin glutted Huminik with questions for the next several minutes, many of them quite personal.

Yes, Huminik replied, he had a wife named Alice, four young children, and he lived in Camp Springs, Maryland, a nearby suburb of Washington.

"Why, isn't that a coincidence," trilled Revin. "Do you know that I also live near there—at Silver Spring."

Huminik's reaction to that, as recalled in an interview with the author: "I think I did a double-take when I heard he lived so near to me."

Even as he spoke with Revin the cogs in Huminik's mind churned, trying to make sense of this stranger who had descended upon him so suddenly and completely. This meeting had all the earmarks of casualness and accident. Yet Huminik couldn't help wondering about the Russian's presence at the technical society gathering.

He didn't have to wonder for long. The Soviet diplomat came to the point at once.

"I'd like you to be a good fellow and help me obtain some information and material which I am sure you will be able to get without much trouble. Can I count on you?"

Revin looked Huminik in the eye with a steady gaze as he waited for his reaction.

Huminik was flustered at the approach, completely lacking in subtlety.

"What information?" he stammered.

"In particular," Revin said, keeping his voice deliberately low in the crowded meeting hall, "we would like to find out about certain aspects of American technology in the iron and steel industry."

Huminik looked puzzled. "But you shouldn't have any trouble obtaining such data," he snapped. "All you've got to do is go to the Government Printing Office and ask for pamphlets and brochures on the subject."

Revin stared at Huminik in prolonged silence, then broke into a toothy grin.

"Of course, it is the way to do it," the Russian said airily. "I know that. But I have good and valid reason to ask you to perform that little service for me. I cannot talk anymore now. Allow me to invite you to dinner, perhaps next Monday evening?"

He looked at the engineer with a plaintive, almost pleading expression, all the while grinning. It was such an incongruous play of facial features that Huminik might have laughed—if the whole thing hadn't been so deadly serious.

"I suppose that's all right," Huminik said. "I don't have any pressing business coming up Monday evening that I can think of."

"Good, good," Revin said. "Then we shall meet at the Blair Mansion Inn. Is that all right with you?"

Huminik nodded.

"Let us say seven o'clock," the Soviet diplomat suggested. "I shall make the reservation."

"Okay," Huminik said and shook hands again with Revin, who began edging away slowly.

"If you don't mind," the Russian said over his shoulder, "I think I shall browse a bit through the hall." He bowed slightly as he stepped back, then turned and walked away.

As Revin disappeared into the crowd, Huminik had no difficulty reaching a judgment about his first encounter with a Soviet diplomat.

"It was a blatant attempt by a Soviet Embassy official to recruit me into the world of espionage," Huminik recalls. "I knew the score—that the request for U.S. Government Printing Office literature would only be the beginning, and once I delivered that material there'd be requests for more important data, which I might even have to steal.

"I was convinced at that very moment that Revin was a genuine Soviet spy . . ."

And with that thought, Huminik hurried out of the American Association of University Women headquarters and went to his car.

Thirty-five minutes later he was home—and on the phone to the FBI. Early that evening he met with agents and recited every step of the approach and conversation with Valentin Revin. He told of how he had consented to meet the Soviet diplomat at dinner the following Monday night.

"Our advice is to keep the date," one of the agents told Huminik. "And bring him the material he asked for. In fact, we'll get it for you so that you won't have to be bothered."

Huminik was instructed further to conduct his dealings with Revin as he did the first time: being friendly but coy. He also was to pretend to need money.

"If you indicate that you're not too well off financially, he'll take it for granted that you'll be willing to do anything for money," Huminik was told. "You'll be able to draw him out and be able to find out what he's really after."

For the youthful engineer the assignment was a challenge he readily accepted. He understood clearly when the agents pointed out how important his role was. Everything must resolve about Huminik's skill in keeping Revin—or whoever else might be assigned to deal with him in the future—believing in his sincerity, as well as in his ability to perform for the Soviets.

This was an extremely sensitive mission. He would have to provide the FBI with accurate reports on every meeting with Revin and on what secrets the Russians asked for.

But Huminik accepted. "I was anxious," he says. "It was an opportunity to do something very important for my country."

And as he took the assignment, he also agreed to abide by the restriction the FBI imposes on every double-agent. Huminik couldn't tell anyone what he was doing, not his partners in the engineering firm, not his closest friends and associates, not even his wife.

The following Monday, Huminik went to the Blair Mansion Inn promptly at seven P.M. and found Revin waiting in the lobby of the main entrance on Eastern Avenue.

"You are a man of your word, and very prompt," the Soviet diplomat greeted him. Revin took him by the arm and escorted him to the door of the dining room. The headwaiter had a table ready.

During dinner, Huminik took out a small packet from his inside jacket pocket and placed it on the table beside Revin. The Russian diplomat looked at the paper parcel and smiled pleasantly.

"You obtained the information, I see," he said slowly. "Did you encounter any difficulty?"

"None at all," Huminik said easily. "You could have done the same thing. But I was happy to be of service."

Before dinner was over, Revin gave Huminik another assignment. This time he wanted general information on the country's chemical industry. He asked Huminik to meet him with the data on the second Monday of the following month at the Hot Shoppe in the Marriott Motor Hotel on Route 29, at the Key Bridge, just over the Potomac from the Georgetown University campus.

Again the requested information was routine. This time the FBI not only procured pamphlets and brochures from the U.S. Government Printing Office, but also supplied some voluminous but not-too-secretive reports from the American Society of Chemical Engineers. The G-men reasoned that if Huminik could begin impressing the Russians with his ability to deliver, they might come to the point of what they were really looking for a lot sooner.

The trick worked. At the very next get-together, which was in the Sirloin and Saddle Room of the Hot Shoppe, Revin took the thick bundle of papers passed to him and fingered them with vivid delight. His curiosity compelled him to examine the contents right there at the table.

"This is marvelous," he said after scanning some of the papers. "I see you have some very excellent sources." Then came the turn the FBI had expected.

"You are involved in work on the moon project, is that not right?" Revin said. His voice was barely above a whisper.

Huminik stared blankly at the ceiling for a moment.

"How do you know this?" he asked. Actually Huminik wasn't startled that Revin knew of his connection with lunar study and exploration work. The FBI had alerted him to expect the Russians to know more about him, his family, his business, his financial situation, and even the work he was doing, than anyone else might conceivably know.

Huminik returned his gaze from the ceiling to Revin and broke into a smile. The Russian smiled back.

"I've surprised you, haven't I," he said with seeming satisfaction. "I know a few things about you, my friend. That is why we are here together. What you have done for us so far is only the preliminary effort. There are ahead of us much bigger things. I do not say you will become a millionaire, but there will be adequate compensation."

He studied Huminik for a few silent seconds.

"What I would like to do," Revin said, "is to throw some business your way. I shall talk with my government to buy your company's products. I am sure I can arrange it. You should profit handsomely."

Huminik pretended to be pleased.

"John," Revin said in a serious, measured tone, "we are after all the information that can be obtained on the American Surveyor moon project. I need not tell you of its importance to us. We are the leaders in space exploration. We sent up the first Sputnik and we are about to send up many Cosmonauts into the heavens. We intend to be first on the moon.

"Our scientists are already at work on the lunar project, but they must know what the Americans are doing. We know they are behind us, perhaps two years, perhaps more. We want to keep that distance between us—and you can help."

Revin kept his eyes on Huminik to detect his reaction.

"Just what type of information do you want me to try and get for you?" Huminik asked, deliberately injecting a conspiratorial tone into his voice to put the Russian at ease.

Revin replied that the Soviet Union was having problems with miniaturization; its scientific equipment was, for the most part, bulky. That added an unwanted weight factor to Russian payloads and, in turn, demanded larger, more powerful rockets.

"We must find out how the Americans are manufacturing their radio equipment, their television cameras, the other instruments which will be put in the Surveyor."

Revin paused, lighted a cigarette and ordered another round of after-dinner drinks.

"But most important," he went on, "are the specifics about the spacecraft itself. We've got to know how it is being engineered and what its capabilities are. The Soviet Union must know this to surpass the United States effort long before it is made."

Huminik pointed out that the Surveyor program was still in infancy, that it would be several years before it became operational. And by then many of the specifications could change radically. It was academic, but Huminik was trying to show good intentions to convince Revin of his sincerity.

"I know all that," Revin said sharply. "What I am telling you is that we must know step-by-step just what the Americans are doing at every stage of development, so we can do better."

Revin made known just what he expected Huminik to deliver at the next get-together—in a month.

"Get the estimated time of completion of the space vehicle, the projected weight, and a general list of the scientific equipment it will be expected to carry aboard to the moon," Revin directed.

The information was still elementary in many respects, much of it already in the public domain. Had Revin subscribed regularly to *Mechanix Illustrated* or any of a number of other first-rate scientific magazines or periodicals, he could have found many of the answers to his questions. Undoubtedly, Revin—or certainly other members of his scientific group back at the Embassy—must have read those articles and prepared voluminous reports for Moscow.

But in delegating Huminik to come up with information they probably already had, the Russians were setting him up for more important chores—gathering facts and figures on the spacecraft and its instrumentation which would never be published and for obvious reasons would probably remain classified. Huminik was able to deliver a generous portion of the data Revin had asked for at the next meeting, once more in a Washington area restaurant.

The confrontation between Revin and Huminik and the delivery of information became almost a ritual after this. Revin established a routine which obligated Huminik to supply reports on the moon probe at least once every month. During the first year of the conspiracy, Russian requests occasionally got complicated. Revin would ask for information that sometimes was impossible to supply without imperiling the security of the program.

In instances when such information couldn't be provided, Huminik made "partial deliveries," as authorities put it, "and stalled for time on the rest of the order."

"The idea was to keep the Russians on the hook," Huminik told the author. "I'd have to apologize for not being able to come up with all the data the Russians wanted, and I'd keep them dangling on the end of my string by making promises that I'd try to have it for them the next time around or the time after that."

Although Huminik was unable to fill all the orders fully, the Russians always seemed pleased with what he was giving them. They never let their disappointment show. Nor did Huminik ever receive a complaint that the information—the "doctored" information, that is—had been found to be worthless. Evidently the National Aeronautics and Space Administration had done its job *faultlessly* in faking the documents.

Several other Soviets joined the conspiracy after a time. In every case, however, the conspirators came under the FBI's scrutiny. With telephoto cameras poised in strategic observation posts to watch every meeting between Huminik and Revin, or the other Russians, and with eavesdropping equipment secreted under many of the restaurant tables where they frequently met and dined, the FBI gathered a documented, running account of the continuing plot as it progressed through 1963, then 1964 and into 1965.

The modus operandi of the conspiracy remained unchanged for the first three and a half years. Then all at once it began to take on the cloak-and-dagger overtones of a familiar spy case that the FBI had broken a decade before. That was the attempt by a combination of Soviet agents—Aleksandr Petrovich Kovalev, Second Secretary of the Soviet Delegation to the United Nations and a graduate of the Soviet School for Espionage and Sabotage in Moscow, and Igor Aleksandrovich Amosov, an assistant naval attaché at the Soviet Embassy in Washington—to steal the Sperry bombsight through an engineer employed by a large electronics firm on Long Island.

The engineer, whose name was never revealed by the FBI, had become a double-agent, just as Huminik was now, and participated in a series of clandestine meetings with the Russians during 1952 which involved "dead drops" on out-of-the-way streets on Long Island, a system of marking pages of a telephone book in a Brooklyn restaurant to indicate when delivery of secret data was made, a series of complicated recognition signal systems (including the placing of a banana peel on a traffic light stanchion in Central Park), and microfilm photographs of documents that couldn't be removed from the grounds of the Long Island electronics plant.

Once the conspiracy in which John Huminik starred as the hero approached its fourth anniversary, the similarities of the earlier Sperry bombsight case sprouted with surprising suddenness . . .

First, just as Kovalev had pushed the Long Island engineer onto

Amosov as his new contact, so did Revin shuffle Huminik off on another Soviet agent, stepping into the background himself.

The FBI is certain this practice is employed when the Soviets feel that the margin of safety for one of their agents has diminished, and this real or imagined fear makes them pull their man back and put a new one in his place. Whether the Kremlin spy machine had reason to believe Revin had been discovered, and decided he should be supplanted by a new face to avoid further detection, is something only the Russians know.

Huminik continued to deal with the new Soviet agent just as he had with Revin.

The FBI has not identified this second Kremlin spy, nor the others who did business occasionally with Huminik. Nor did Huminik say who those others were.

"The FBI and the State Department have their reasons for maintaining secrecy," Huminik told the author. "I cannot reveal who they are, although I know them quite well."

In all probability the FBI is still watching these Russians, hoping to catch them in some other espionage activity.

There came a time in the 1952 Sperry bombsight case when Amosov dropped out of the picture as suddenly as he had become a part of it, and Kovalev, his predecessor, again took over as before in dealing with the Long Island engineer. It was no different in the Surveyor spy case.

It happened in early 1965. Just as mysteriously as he had dropped out, Revin came back and replaced the second Soviet official who had been Huminik's contact. And all their dealings again took on the pattern of the past—even the promises to repay Huminik with that still-elusive Soviet contract for the Value Engineering Company.

Then came fall, 1965, and Revin called Huminik unexpectedly. He asked him to meet him in the Four Georgias Restaurant in Georgetown. At dinner that night of September 29, Revin told the double-agent:

"I am leaving next week for Moscow. While I am there I will work out that contract I have been promising to get you. I shall see you when I return in a few weeks."

Revin came back Thanksgiving week and soon after summoned Huminik to another dinner get-together at the Embassy Steak House on Connecticut Avenue. He was sad-faced as he sat at the table with the American. Revin had come with disappointing news —he wasn't able to arrange the contract.

For Huminik it made no difference. He had sold his interest in Value and taken a position with Melpar, a division of the Westing-house Corporation, to work on missile production and defense design work.

Revin was aware of these changes and Huminik's connection with Westinghouse appeared to please the Russian. Revin let it be known that Huminik could expect immediate compensation for all further efforts. Up to now Huminik had gotten not a cent—merely the promise of profits on the contract that never materialized.

"I will pay you cash for the material you give to me from now on," was how Revin said it to Huminik. "I will begin payments next month."

But that wasn't all. Beginning next month, Revin explained, there must be a change in procedure. Although he'd continue to meet Huminik for dinner, it would be "strictly social," as he put it. He would no longer take delivery of information at the restaurants.

"You will leave the material at certain places that I will designate," Revin said.

It was the Sperry bombsight case once again. With his system of "dead drops," Revin also introduced the device of marking certain pages of telephone books at specified booths in the Washington area. Huminik must go there, look up the page he'd been alerted in advance to check, and find the notation for the time and place of the "drop." Then he'd deliver the material.

Revin also instructed Huminik to buy a miniature camera to photograph all secret data transmitted in the future.

"We don't want to get involved any more with bulky papers," Revin said cryptically. "It could be dangerous. From now on, just take pictures and deliver the undeveloped negative where I tell you to bring it. I will take care of the rest. Just wrap the film in black waterproof paper."

Then came the final, shocking order from Revin.

"We want you to buy a miniature tape recorder to wear under your jacket. With this device we want you to record the conversations you have with Pentagon officials. We know you have occasion to discuss important matters with the Defense Department people. Record those conversations. We believe they will be helpful to us."

When he advised the FBI of the sudden new, bold pattern of subversion that Revin had proposed, Huminik was told to "play along." The FBI helped him buy the miniature camera and tape recorder and did most of the work involved in picture-taking and "bugging" conversations with the "Defense Department people" in the Pentagon, who, in fact, were FBI agents engaging Huminik in discussions about missiles, the moon probe, and other vital topics. They had all the overtones of being secret, vital conferences—but they were really just so much worthless talk.

However, when Huminik began delivering the films and tapes to the "drops" around Washington, the response from Revin was an ecstatic "bravo." The Russian was elated with the photos and recorded conversations. And, as promised, he promptly rewarded his source with cash. The payments came in envelopes, handed to Huminik in private, sometimes in the washrooms of restaurants, at others in the parking lot of shopping centers on the outskirts of the capital or across the Potomac in Alexandria or Arlington.

All in all, between the fall of 1965 and mid-summer of 1966, Revin paid more than five thousand dollars to Huminik for material delivered to the "drops." Material that, as the FBI put it, was "absolutely worthless."

Yet despite the claim that the information was of no account, the

Soviet Union on February 3, 1966, soft-landed the first Luna on the moon and televised those historic close-up photos of the lunar landscape back to earth. That was fully four months before the United States put its own Surveyor on the moon.

It would be grossly unfair to the Soviet Union and its own remarkable and dedicated scientists to speculate that any of the engineering know-how that went into their Luna vehicle came from American sources. Yet isn't it entirely conceivable that other Soviet agents posted in the Embassy in Washington—or at the United Nations in New York—could have gathered secret information on the Surveyor program from a source or sources other than Huminik, and forwarded the data to Moscow? Still, we have no proof of this.

The State Department finally shut off Revin on September 1, 1966, when James W. Bratt, the department's acting director for Soviet affairs, informed Alexander I. Zinchuk, Soviet chargé d'affaires, that Valentin Revin was persona non grata and ordered the diplomat's immediate departure.

The next day, Robert J. McCloskey, the State Department's press officer, announced the action to newsmen and issued this official statement:

"Yesterday a representative of the Soviet Embassy was called into the department and handed a note requesting the immediate departure from this country of Third Secretary of the Soviet Embassy, Valentin A. Revin.

"Revin was engaged in activities clearly incompatible with his diplomatic status during his assignment in the United States—attempting to obtain classified information from an American citizen in return for large sums of money.

"The FBI thwarted these attempts.

"According to the diplomatic list, Revin was one of seven science officers presently attached to the Embassy."

That was the extent of the statement and beyond this the State

Department was silent on details of the case. This official secrecy contrasted sharply with the publicity given to the previous spy case —the attempt by Czechoslovak diplomats to "bug" the State Department.

But the FBI touched upon a few details in a later announcement, although it didn't dwell at any great length on any of them.

Both the State Department and FBI withheld Huminik's identity, as they do in all cases involving Americans who become double-agents. But the cloak of anonymity didn't last long. The Washington press corps soon learned about John Huminik and went to him for his story. He told it, but sparsely.

"If you want further details," he said, "you will have to get them from the FBI."

Huminik expressed the same reluctance to discuss his experience with this author—until it was made clear to him that it would be reported in a book to be called *Red Spies in Washington*. Then he consented to tell only what he believed would not interfere with the FBI's continuing work against espionage.

Huminik spoke glowingly of the FBI.

"As far as I'm concerned," he said, "the FBI runs one of the tightest ships I've ever seen. The agents there are some of the most hard-working and sophisticated people I've ever known. They're first-class citizens, the unsung heroes of our country.

"During the time I was with them, they did nothing that was illegal or un-American. They guided me at every turn, although there were times obviously when I had to go it alone.

"Little did I suspect when it started that it would last five long years. But it was a once-in-a-lifetime chance for an American to do something for his country. And if I had it to do over again, I'd do it—the same way."

If Huminik has any regret about the case, it is only because Valentin Revin was deported so abruptly. Huminik had woven a remarkable rapport with the Russian in the years that he played a cat-and-mouse game with him. In the last days of the conspiracy, Huminik began to see the signs of change in Revin. Signs that had Huminik almost convinced Revin was ready to defect!

"The way of life here was winning Revin over," Huminik said. "He had been here so long that he literally had fallen in love with the country."

Actually, the Moscow-born Revin had first come to the United States in 1958 as an exchange student at the University of California at Berkeley. The following summer Revin served two months as a guide and interpreter at the Soviet Exhibition in New York City's Coliseum. A short while later he was assigned to the Embassy in Washington.

And not long after that—regardless of what feelings he might ultimately hold for the United States—Revin began his activities in espionage.

But being a spy evidently was not in Revin's character. At least his heart didn't seem to be in it. Science was his field and he had confided in Huminik that scientific study was what he really yearned to pursue.

Orders from the Kremlin, however, thwarted that ambition and made Valentin Revin what he said he never cared to be.

Now, on the afternoon of Wednesday, September 7—five days after his expulsion was ordered—Revin walked out for the last time from the pleasant apartment at New Hampshire West Court in Silver Spring, which had been a happy home for him and his family the last few years. With him were his wife Aleksandra, thirty-five, and their three-year-old daughter, Olga. They were bound for the Soviet Union.

A shuttle flight from National Airport in Washington took them to Kennedy Airport in New York to make connections with an Air France jetliner for Paris, first leg on their hop back to Moscow.

Revin, attired in a smart blue tweed suit, white shirt, and powder-blue tie, was all smiles as he stepped off the Washington plane and made his way with his wife and daughter to the Air France lounge to wait for the transatlantic flight.

All during the hour until boarding time. Revin chatted amiably with a group of Soviet attachés who had come out from the U.N. Mission to see him off. He didn't seem to have a care in the world.

But when it was time to board the plane, a reporter caught Revin as he started up the ramp.

"Mr. Revin," called out the reporter, "do you expect a hero's welcome when you arrive home—or an assignment in Siberia?"

"I have no comment," Revin said in a thin, sinking tone.

But with that the smile disappeared. For the first time he seemed worried. The question apparently had brought Valentin A. Revin face-to-face with reality at last. Perhaps it made him wonder, as others were wondering now—

What can the future be in the Soviet Union for a spy who failed to bring home the prize—our Surveyor on the moon?

14

From the Age of Innocence to the Age of Suspicion to the Age of Confusion

> The necessity of procuring good Intelligence is apparent and need not be further urged. All that remains for me to add, is, that you keep the whole matter as secret as possible. For upon Secrecy, Success depends in most Enterprizes of the kind, and for want of it, they are generally defeated, however, well planned and promising a favourable issue.

When George Washington wrote these words to Colonel Elias Dayton on July 26, 1777, the Continental Army was in throes of battle with the Redcoats and the future of the United States of America was in the balance. Nearly two hundred years later, Washington's statement is still applicable. But what was then a mere admonition to an officer on the field of battle and to a few hundred of his men is today a standing order to hundreds of thousands of agents in the employ of intelligence services of various nations around the world.

This book is primarily the story of Soviet espionage in the United

States. However, the number of cases described here and the increasing number of Soviet plots uncovered during the last two decades should not be construed as the result of a proliferation of Kremlin activity on our shores—such activity having existed in considerable strength for nearly forty years. Instead, our growing awareness of Soviet espionage is a direct result of our more sophisticated counterintelligence techniques—by the Federal Bureau of Investigation and the Central Intelligence Agency.

While the American populace is shocked at each unmasking of a Soviet spy, the mass of disclosures in the past few years has tended to dull our sense of danger and lull us into an attitude where the business of Soviet subversion in the United States is an accepted fact of life, not unlike the Cold War.

Even the story of a United States Army colonel stationed in the Pentagon offices of the Joint Chiefs of Staff who was arrested and confessed he spied for the Soviets failed to summon the strength in many of us to imagine the implications of this penetration into the high councils of our Government.

Yet there was a time in our recent past when Americans were profoundly shocked and angered—even frightened—by the smashing of a Soviet espionage plot. But the mood of the people in those times was different.

We were then, all of us, living in the Age of Innocence.

For those who don't remember Elizabeth Bentley, Whittaker Chambers, William Remington, and Alger Hiss, it is important to know that they and their constellation of fellow-travelers precipitated a sobriety and realism in the American consciousness never before evident.

All of them became the principals in a drama of treason that purportedly was committed in the highest places and shook up American opinion as few events in our history have done.

All of them shocked the country into an awareness of the corrosive double political life that could exist under the surface of respectability; and they helped bring an end to the Age of Innocence, particularly among those who found it staggering to conceive that the Russians, our war allies, could be so evil as to spy on us.

Until then we had learned nothing from lessons of the past because the past had offered us little, if anything, to learn. As a people in the world community of nations we were limited and pragmatic. We had always been enamoured of our great strength as a nation. Traditionally, we were held by an egregious naiveté rooted in our claim to greatness. This was a certitude sustained since the Revolution because of our success as a democratic society. We were never chafed either by fear of military conquest or ideological defeat by another nation.

On the eve of World War II, we were still a nation not given to suspicion or fear of an enemy. We showed little concern over the rise of Nazi Germany and imperialistic Japan—until the threat of those nations became imminent. To a great extent we were oblivious until the Japanese sneak attack on Pearl Harbor and the Philippines.

Then we awakened and realized in our profound shock how vulnerable we really were.

We were told that Japan's devastating air raids of that December 7, 1941, were the product of effective espionage which had enabled Nippon's intelligence operatives to gather accurate information on our fleet and air force concentrations at Pearl Harbor and Manila.

We were also told that those attacks pointed up our own great weakness and inadequacy for intelligence responsibilities. Until that time our own intelligence activities had been limited to a narrow perimeter. And whatever those activities were, they were totally inept.

Until then we had engaged only in the *overt* collection of foreign information, conducted exclusively by the State Department through its diplomats and employees on foreign soil. They derived their intelligence, for the most part, from newspapers, radio, books, technical journals, and those official government reports that they were able to view. The information was openly available in the capitals and cities of the nations where our embassies and consulates were situated. We took that information as it came merely because it was there to take. It helped us keep abreast of developments—or so we were led to believe.

In the same way, diplomats of foreign powers assigned to embassies in Washington and consulates in other major cities in the United States gathered information that enabled them to keep an eye on America's military, economic, and social growth.

But there was a difference. The countries which had access to information here were able to gather far greater amounts than our people overseas, simply because the United States gave visiting diplomats freedom to travel. Our own emissaries in many of their bases abroad, greatly restricted in their excursions, were handicapped in their intelligence efforts.

During the 1930s, for example, Hitler's Germany, Mussolini's Italy, Tojo's Japan, and Stalin's Russia built powerful military machines behind our backs because they took extraordinary precautions to seal off vast areas of their countries where the buildup was occurring. Our diplomats—our eyes and ears in those lands—had no certain knowledge of the fighting strength being developed behind the wall of secrecy.

While our own democratic leniency had committed us to suffer this imbalance in *overt* intelligence capability, we were handicapped to an even greater degree by the existence of another force in espionage—the *clandestine,* the gathering of information by devious means through undercover agents, or spies.

During the 1930s and in all the years before that period going back to the Revolution, the United States had no tolerance for clandestine espionage. And although our military forces had the structure for clandestine intelligence activity, it was used merely to provide military commanders with enemy strength and movements on the field of battle during wartime.

In peacetime this arm of intelligence was restrained, with the United States relying solely on diplomats to provide the State Department and the Armed Forces with intelligence data about foreign powers. Yet nations such as Germany, Japan, Italy, and the Soviet Union were known to have infiltrated the United States with their undercover agents. They came as immigrants or travelers—in some instances they were smuggled in—to pilfer our most important secrets in national defense and foreign policy.

The tragic aspect was that the United States had no effective counterintelligence force against such spies.

The enemy was able to learn much about us, while we found out comparatively little about the enemy.

That we survived the attack at Pearl Harbor was a tribute to our traditional might and force and our iron determination to win despite the staggering devastation of the sneak punch.

It was only after our entry into World War II that we opened our eyes wide to intelligence as a craft of formidable importance and to the need to have it managed by professional craftsmen.

We entered the arena of espionage in earnest when President Franklin D. Roosevelt summoned William J. Donovan to Washington to organize the Office of Strategic Services, which served as our premier military intelligence force until war's end. Then with the onset of the emerging political struggle with Communism and its absorption of nations brooding over their ruins of war, America was compelled to meet a new challenge. The Iron Curtain had been lowered. We had to penetrate it for our own security.

"The war taught us this lesson," stated President Harry S Truman, "that we had to collect intelligence in a manner that would make the information available where it was needed and when it was wanted, in an intelligent and understandable form."

So in 1947 the President submitted to a Republican-controlled

Congress his proposal for the creation of a peacetime central intelligence agency as a permanent arm of government and a mechanism for coordinating intelligence to provide the President, the Secretary of State, and Secretary of Defense with a single reasoned analysis of factors and situations bearing on our national security. Truman made certain the Central Intelligence Agency, as it was christened, was equipped to deal with the Communist tactics of "coercion, subterfuge, and political infiltration."

No one then thought the CIA would one day proliferate into an organization with its own army, merchant marine, air force—and with the capability of sending fighting men and equipment any place on earth. Nor did anyone envision a 5000-man branch of government with more than 200,000 "spies" on its global payroll, and an expenditure of nearly five billion dollars a year.

It was only 1947 and as yet the vast majority of the populace was totally unaware of the widespread espionage activity being consigned to the CIA. At that time it was hardly reasonable to expect the public to understand, let alone support an arm of government such as the CIA whose primary mission was to spy on other nations. That was a time when—in spite of Pearl Harbor—we were acquainted with only one type of spy—the fictional character we had read about in books or viewed in movies.

We had no knowledge that our own country had been invaded long ago, by spies from the Soviet Union and its satellite countries —and that we not only had to stop or slow them down, but to spy on them as a matter of our own security and survival as a nation.

We were still living in the Age of Innocence.

But the end of that era of naiveté was rapidly approaching . . .

As already suggested, the people began awakening to the full meaning of treason and espionage in early 1948, after the names of Elizabeth Bentley, Whittaker Chambers, William Remington, and Alger Hiss were thrust upon the American scene.

Long-fermenting rumors about treason and espionage and the possible involvement of persons in high Government posts compelled House and Senate committees to hold hearings on how far the supposed Communist conspiracy extended.

The hearings began with Elizabeth Bentley, a plump, brown-haired woman of forty, an idealistic former Vassar girl who had been reared in a devout Congregationalist household in Milford, Connecticut. She went before the committees and told of how she had begun stalking through the jungle of subversion as long ago as the early 1930s, not many months after President Roosevelt had given Josef Stalin the keys to the Soviet Embassy in Washington and the first Kremlin spies came over in the guise of diplomats.

She told of how for two years she traveled every other weekend from New York to Washington as a courier to pick up documents collected by two groups of Communists in Government service, one allegedly headed by Nathan Gregory Silvermaster, director of the War Assets Administration, and the other purportedly under the direction of Victor Perlo, a Treasury Department analyst.

The mention of these names alone stunned the country.

Then Elizabeth Bentley told the finer details of the alleged conspiracy and how she was enmeshed in espionage by a Soviet agent named Jacob Rasin, alias Golos, who became her lover.

When Jacob Rasin had died in Elizabeth Bentley's arms in their bedroom on Thanksgiving Day, 1943, her existence ground almost to a stop. Communism, she soon concluded, was only "a dirty racket and not an idealistic movement."

Her "good old New England conscience" and the fact that "gangster type" Soviet agents had taken over her sources of information in Washington compelled her to break with Communism. She went to the FBI offices in New Haven, Connecticut, and there stepped from the purposeful obscurity of the secret agent into the equally purposeful—and much more dangerous—role of the double-agent.

Continuing as a courier in the service of the Kremlin between Washington and the New York "drop" under the alias Helen Johnson, Elizabeth Bentley supplied the FBI with the names of thirty-seven employees of Government agencies and wartime boards—including Silvermaster and Perlo—with whom she said she dealt in the capital.

As the FBI worked to gather evidence—evidence with which the Justice Department could go to court and obtain convictions—a strange development took shape. Although the G-men had been on the investigation nearly five years, they had not been able to solidify cases against even a single individual—at least not solidly enough for the indictments necessary for prosecution.

Yet suddenly the FBI was rudely bypassed by the Congressional committees which announced their intentions to investigate the "Communist conspiracy" and certain Americans believed to be involved in the plot. Very soon afterward the committees launched their hearings and trumpeted the names of those suspected of espionage. There was much flag-waving and much wild ballyhoo. Charges were scattered in every direction like buckshot, seemingly in the hope that an occasional accusation would hit.

It was quite a contrast to the careful, reserved, meticulous respect for facts which the FBI had maintained. The FBI had never made any wild charges or rash statements. Nobody was accidentally hurt by the smear of a Red brush. The FBI wanted only facts and evidence against the thirty-seven suspected Government employees.

But the Congressional hearings went at it differently. They opened with a frightening tone as Elizabeth Bentley recalled the story of how she had received information on the production of aircraft and armaments, on a project to make synthetic rubber out of garbage, and on the projected data for the invasion of Europe, among much else.

Then she rattled off the names of the thirty-seven, telling the

Congressmen that Harry Dexter White, President Truman's Assistant Secretary of the Treasury, was her "most important source of
information." This charge had repercussions in the White House—
and also in the office of FBI Director J. Edgar Hoover.

President Truman said the hearings at which Elizabeth Bentley
appeared were "a red herring" meant to divert attention from the
failure of the Republican-controlled 80th Congress to legislate
against inflation.

Congressional investigators countered that the President in 1946
had received FBI reports, largely based on Elizabeth Bentley's disclosures, that implicated White in espionage—yet the White House
"promoted" him to the position of United States member on the
executive board of the International Monetary Fund.

White resigned from the post unexpectedly and without explanation in 1947, before the spy scandals exploded in the capital. Following Elizabeth Bentley's startling testimony, he appeared before
the House Subcommittee on Un-American Activities and denied
the allegations under oath. Three days later, Harry Dexter White
was dead of a heart attack.

Truman then stated publicly that White had been given the Fund
post so the FBI could continue its investigation without attracting
suspicion. FBI Director Hoover denied this.

Although Elizabeth Bentley's testimony helped to convict eleven
Communist Party leaders in 1949 for conspiring to advocate the
overthrow of the Government, her accusations alone were not suffi-
cient for a Federal grand jury to hand up indictments for spying
against any of the thirty-seven persons she implicated.

However, William Remington was convicted of perjury for testi-
fying that he had never been a member of the Communist Party,
Elizabeth Bentley having testified that she had collected dues from
him for two years.

Presumably in return for her cooperation, she herself escaped
prosecution for espionage and soon after dropped out of sight. She

drifted into obscurity as a teacher at schools in various parts of the country and on December 3, 1963, she died of an abdominal tumor.

The Whittaker Chambers-Alger Hiss espionage sensations which broke almost at the same time as the scandals touched off by Elizabeth Bentley, stirred an even more potent spy stew for Congressional investigators. The recitals here involved not only Chambers' account of his own admitted role as a courier for a Soviet spy ring in the years just preceding World War II, but his accusations against Alger Hiss, a man who had risen rapidly in government and statecraft and seemed at the very crest of a brilliant career—until shot down by the charges.

Chambers swore that Hiss fed him U.S. Government documents in 1937 and 1938 from his high-ranking desk in the State Department for relay to Russian spies. Hiss did this, Chambers swore, because Hiss, too, was a Communist.

The charges were earthshaking. A student of world affairs, a man of many diplomatic assignments, a graduate of New Deal Washington, which had become the capital of Harry Truman's Fair Deal, Hiss had played a substantial part in organizing the United Nations, and earlier was among the small group of advisers who accompanied President Roosevelt to the "Big Three" Yalta Conference.

About the time Hiss was starting up the ladder to high places, Chambers was starting down—into the shadowy Communist underground. But it was during those very days, Chambers testified, that he met Hiss, found him a Communist comrade and, by extension, a source for secret State Department documents.

Hiss had begun his rise to positions of governmental responsibility in 1936 when he went to the Justice Department as a special attorney, and later in the year became an aide to Assistant Secretary of State Francis B. Sayre.

Not long after, Chambers related, he told Hiss about a Colonel Boris Bykov, who was "head of the underground apparatus with which I was then connected, and with which Hiss was connected." Hiss met Bykov at a Brooklyn theater in January or February, 1937, according to Chambers, who claimed he was also present. The three then went to a dimly lighted Chinatown restaurant and across a table there the colonel got Hiss to agree to obtain the secrets from the State Department.

Hiss, who denied ever taking the papers or ever knowing Colonel Bykov, was accused by Chambers of delivering State Department documents in wholesale fashion from 1937 into 1938, mostly reports on Germany and Japan, material that the Soviet Union, anxiously watching the rise of Germany on her west and Japan on her east, would have been interested in.

In April, 1938, after taking a post with the National Research Project, under the Works Progress Administration, Chambers said he finally came to regard Communism as evil, quit the Party, and set out to atone for what he had tried to do to his country by putting the nation on guard against Communists.

Chambers said he went to Hiss's home and tried to persuade him to follow that lead. Hiss assertedly refused.

In 1939, Chambers decided he had to reveal the story of the Communist underground in Washington. He tried but was unable to see President Roosevelt, then as an alternative went to A. A. Berle, Jr., the Assistant Secretary of State, and told him. Chambers didn't confess his role as a courier in espionage but merely his former membership in the Communist Party and some details about the existence of the Red underground.

Nothing happened and in 1942 Chambers decided to deal with the FBI. He gave them information about Harry Dexter White, whom he characterized as a possible Communist and "certainly a fellow-traveler" in the Hiss "apparatus."

Whatever the FBI thought about that information on Harry

Dexter White, it certainly must have thought more of it a year later when Elizabeth Bentley came to them with what amounted to corroboration of Chambers' charges. For the next four years the FBI gave no indication that it was investigating these charges. But some time in 1946, Hiss was summoned to the office of Secretary of State James F. Byrnes and, as Hiss put it:

"Byrnes said several members of Congress were preparing to make statements on the floor of Congress that I was a Communist. He asked me if I were and I said I was not. He said, 'This is a serious matter. I think all the stories center from the FBI . . . I think you would be well advised to go directly to the FBI and offer yourself for a very full inquiry and investigation.'

"I immediately went . . . I recited every organization I had ever been connected with to see if they could possibly be of any significance to them. They asked me if I knew certain individuals . . . they did not mention the name Chambers, I am quite sure."

On February 1, 1947, Hiss left the Government and assumed the twenty-thousand-dollar-a-year presidency of the Carnegie Endowment for International Peace. In May, two FBI agents called on him to ask if he knew certain persons, including Whittaker Chambers. This, said Hiss, was the first time he'd heard the name and he didn't connect it with a "George Crosley" he knew as a writer in Washington who came to him for material on the Senate munitions inquiry early in the 1930s, and who had also rented his Washington apartment.

Chambers admitted he had used the name "George Crosley" during those days.

As August approached, the country braced for an upcoming event of immense proportions—the House Committee on Un-American Activities announced it would hold hearings to determine the extent of Communist espionage and infiltration into Government.

One of the witnesses to be subpoenaed was Whittaker Chambers, who had testified in secret to House investigators. By this time Chambers, who had joined the staff of *Time* Magazine in 1939, was its senior editor at a thirty-thousand-dollar-a-year salary. Although his name then was known mostly to those who took the trouble to glance at *Time*'s masthead, Whittaker Chambers soon would be a household word.

On August 3, the House Committee on Un-American Activities began its hearings, with much of the credit for preparing the stage for Hiss's appearance going to a young Republican Congressman from California and a member of the committee named Richard M. Nixon.

The country, of course, needed a hero and Nixon was as good a candidate as any to slip into knight's armor, mount a white steed, and ride forth to slay the treacherous Red dragon that had all at once uncoiled across the breadth of the land.

Nothing could have been more urgent. The Cold War had set in. The Republican Party was trying to emerge from fifteen New Deal and Fair Deal years. The Communist issue had now begun to loom larger than ever.

The Hiss Affair, double-teamed with the Elizabeth Bentley revelations, was all the country needed to create the climate of the times. And where Elizabeth Bentley failed to stir up America's ire against Russians and Communists, Whittaker Chambers succeeded. He crystallized American outrage by going before the House Committee and spilling the incredible and shocking details about his relationship with Hiss—telling of visits to Hiss's home, of having met Mrs. Hiss, and of how he established Hiss's connection with the Communist "underground."

In the course of the exposures, Chambers produced a pile of documents which he said had been stolen from the State Department and other Government files. These were the documents, Chambers said, which Hiss turned over to him—documents that dealt with Germany and Japan, material that Chambers, as a self-described Communist courier, would have been interested in obtaining for the Soviet Union.

One of the papers, a cable from Arthur Bliss Lane, the U.S. Minister to Belgrade, Yugoslavia, discussed the question of a German attack in the Balkans, a subject of particular interest to Russia. Others described Hitler's demands on Austria, conditions in Fascist Spain, and Japanese troop movements, armament, and trade.

Chambers said the documents, which he produced, had been retrieved by himself earlier from their hiding place in the dumbwaiter of a rundown Brooklyn tenement, where he had secreted them in 1938 in his last days as a Communist courier.

This development brought the House investigators to Chambers' farm in Maryland on December 2. Chambers led the probers to a hollowed-out pumpkin. Inside the pumpkin they found five films with two hundred photographs of classified Government documents—one purportedly in Hiss's handwriting and others allegedly prepared on a Woodstock typewriter said to belong to him, but long missing.

On December 6, a Federal grand jury in New York City which had been impaneled earlier by Assistant U.S. Attorney Thomas F. Murphy to study evidence in the case was convened to hear testimony from Chambers and Hiss.

On December 15, the day its term was to expire, the grand jury returned an indictment against Hiss. He was charged with two counts of perjury, for denying he had given any documents to Chambers and for saying he hadn't met Chambers after January 1, 1937, which was months before the admitted Communist courier claimed he'd received the first State Department papers from Hiss.

Hiss was brought to trial on May 31, 1949, in New York's Federal Court in Foley Square with the Government prosecutor labeling the defendant a traitor and expressing regret that he had to be tried only for perjury. No spy charge was possible because the three-year statute of limitations had long passed.

Hiss took the stand and denied Chambers' accusations point by point. He swore that not a single Government secret ever passed from his hands to Chambers, or to any other unauthorized person; he also denied having seen Chambers after January 1, 1937, and told the jury that the man who was trying to ruin him was merely a casual acquaintance.

The defense pounded at Chambers' checkered past and set it against Hiss's positions of honor and trust; Chambers was subjected to a hammering cross-examination during which he admitted he lied under oath in numerous instances—even seven times to the grand jury which indicted Hiss for perjury. But through all the defense pounding, he stuck to his detailed account about Hiss and the others he claimed had supplied him with Government secrets.

Lloyd Paul Stryker, trial counsel for Hiss, provided a surprise when he announced in court that the defense had located the long-missing Woodstock typewriter. Then the claim was made that the typewriter actually had belonged to Chambers.

Prosecutor Murphy introduced the forty-seven documents copied on the Woodstock and had Chambers identify them. Then Murphy charged that Hiss's wife had typed those documents.

Chambers was the cornerstone of the Government's case against Hiss, and when the jury went to deliberate, it had to resolve the ponderous question of which man was lying—were they to believe Chambers' cloak-and-dagger tale of Red infiltration, or Hiss's stubborn denials?

The jury couldn't decide. It returned from its deliberations finally in hopeless deadlock, standing 8 to 4 for conviction.

Hiss went free. But early in 1950, the Government again brought Hiss to trial in New York on the same charges, and this time the jury unanimously decided that Hiss and not Chambers had lied. Hiss was convicted and sentenced to serve five years in the Federal penitentiary.

The U.S. Circuit Court of Appeals unanimously upheld the conviction and the U.S. Supreme Court refused to review the case. On March 22, 1951, Hiss, shackled to a mail thief, was put aboard a U.S. marshal's van and whisked off to Northeastern Federal Penitentiary at Lewisburg, Pennsylvania, to serve his sentence.

Meanwhile, Chambers went about his chores on the farm and subsequently published an autobiography titled *Witness* in 1952, telling his side of the case in most of the 800-odd pages of the book, which soon became a best seller and brought a rich financial return to the man who was down to his last half-dollar when he got his job with *Time* in 1938.

A second book called *Cold Friday,* a 327-page tome comprising mainly a posthumous collection of letters and fragments of a never-finished book, was published in 1964, but it was deemed as nothing more than "a pious attempt to restore and enhance" Chambers' memory.

For now Chambers was dead. His passing was as enigmatic, in a sense, as was much of his life. He died July 9, 1961, at his farm in Westminster, Maryland, but it was only after he was cremated on July 11 that a funeral director gave out the news. It was as if Chambers wanted to be sure that even in death no one would study his brooding, jowl-heavy face for some new insight into the Alger Hiss case.

The case had passed so completely into the half-forgotten history of the 1940s and 1950s that his death served for many persons merely as a surprise reminder that Whittaker Chambers had still been alive until the other day.

Upon Chambers' death, reporters sought out Alger Hiss, who was now living alone on Manhattan's West Side—he had been released from prison in 1954 and afterward wrote a book, made some speaking appearances, became a twenty-thousand-dollar-a-year executive in the comb industry, then quit after three years to become a stationery and printing salesman. He was separated from his wife in 1959.

Hiss declined to comment on the news of Chambers' death, just as Chambers had turned down an invitation years before to do a story for the United Press on Hiss's release from prison.

Chambers had written in his own book: "Throughout the Hiss case, I tried to act by a simple standard: 'He nothing common did, or mean upon that memorable scene.' Apart from my natural feelings, I hold that that course was peculiarly in the public interest . . ."

Whittaker Chambers, even today survives in memory as one of the nation's most incredible paradoxes—a man who lived two lives, first as a traitor, then a patriot of his country.

Although historians must still assess how much this country suffered or benefited from either of those two lives, there seems to be little doubt that Whittaker Chambers—aided by the thunder generated by Elizabeth Bentley—was in large part responsible for the very rapid end to the Age of Innocence.

The change was rapid and drastic. Indeed it stampeded America into the arms of a flag-waving United States Senator named Joseph R. McCarthy, a Republican from Wisconsin. And with his team of bully-boys, America flew headlong into the Age of Suspicion.

This was the period of the 1950s, an era when McCarthy's marauders employed tactics no more refined than Soviet Secret Police Chief Lavrenti Beria's "thumbscrews and confession artists" in the Kremlin. They made the flesh creep and they provoked an atmosphere that made this country the shame and laughingstock of the Western World.

In doing their assessing, historians must also decide who did more harm—the naive innocents who held to the view that Moscow was our friend, or the hysterical disenchanted when they finally saw through the thin veil of the "good guy" draped over the renegade Russian Bear.

The ways in which human beings make history are incalculable. Elizabeth Bentley, Whittaker Chambers, William Remington, and

Alger Hiss, and those others who wallowed in the cesspool of subversion, made it because the people were led to believe they had accomplished enormities of betrayal against their country.

But in proper perspective now, weighing their acts against those of the other Americans subsequently involved in espionage they were, all of them, only amateur informants who helped to establish one incontrovertible truth: the Russian mania for spying can sometimes be sheer stupidity. The Kremlin espionage monster gorged itself with trifling tidbits while it waited for the main course this body of accused and/or admitted traitors was never able to serve up.

In time, however, the others did—after Soviet spy boss Lavrenti Beria recruited more reliable, more competent operatives into the Red intelligence apparatus in this country—people like Julius and Ethel Rosenberg, who passed America's greatest secret, the atom bomb; people like Jack and Myra Sobel, Jacob Albam, Dr. Morton Sobell, Jane and George Zlatovski, Mark Zborowski, and those described in the official cases in this book, who contributed mightily in transmitting intelligence about Uncle Sam's military and defense secrets.

The exposure of spy cases tended to arouse the country's fears and to extend a continuing lease on life to the Age of Suspicion. We were a country now which sincerely believed that we were constantly being spied on. We were also a country that was as yet unaware of our own deeply involved role in spying which we had been doing increasingly since 1947 when President Truman and Congress created the Central Intelligence Agency.

That fact was finally thrust upon the United States and the world with shocking suddenness on May Day, 1960, when America's U-2 spy plane was brought down deep in the heart of the Russian Urals.

That one electrifying incident jolted America's consciousness and at once brought the Age of Suspicion to a dramatic end. Realization that the United States engaged in espionage just as freely as the Soviet Union and that the CIA had created a worldwide network of intelligence that enabled Uncle Sam to keep one jump ahead of real and potential enemies created almost overnight a curious mixture of doubt and dismay, guilt and shame. We, the nation who had cursed and crucified those who spied against us, had suddenly become a nation of spies ourselves.

A new era had dawned—the Age of Confusion.

It was announced—unwittingly—when Premier Nikita Khrushchev gloatingly informed the world of his prize haul—America's super-secret reconnaissance plane and its pilot, Francis Gary Powers, who was alive.

For hours after Khrushchev's bellicose report from Moscow, the CIA and Allen Welsh Dulles, the CIA's director and chief architect of the aerial spy program, kept a discreet silence.

They were abiding by an ancient axiom applying to espionage which is written in, of all places, the *Columbia Encyclopedia,* a publication compiled and edited at Columbia University in New York City, where Dwight David Eisenhower was once president. It goes like this:

"Among nations at peace with each other espionage is never officially admitted, but is almost always practiced."

Yet, while Dulles and his CIA were being silent, Dwight David Eisenhower, who knew the ageless code of espionage as well as any man, apparently decided the awkward position in which the United States had suddenly been thrust called for an immediate change in ground rules governing spy etiquette.

From his office in the White House, the President officially admitted the U-2 flown by pilot Powers was on a spying mission for the United States over Soviet territory. He went even further—admitting that such flights had been going on since 1956.

This bold and meticulously clean breast of the truth was so unprecedented that experts on such matters found little cause to wonder why Khrushchev became so agitated. The Red ruler's fury was climaxed when he single-handedly scuttled the Paris Summit Conference about a fortnight later.

An absolute admission from the President of the United States was probably the last thing in the world the Red boss had expected. Certainly in his wildest dreams Khrushchev would never have contemplated confessing his own country had been engaged in spying on the United States or that Soviet agents and spies—whom we had caught, prosecuted, jailed, even executed—were ever remotely connected with the USSR.

But the bewilderment was not all Khrushchev's. The entire populace of the United States reeled with surprise and dismay as the incident exploded into vituperative Soviet blasts, saber rattling, and beyond—to the frightening precipice of a hot atomic war.

Perhaps no individual was more profoundly shocked by the President's open admission that the United States engaged in spying than America's master of spies himself, Allen Dulles. Dulles, who had been in this country's foreign service since 1916 and had headed America's worldwide intelligence system since 1953, when he became head of the CIA, maintained discreet silence in the face of the President's admission. Privately, Dulles was not reluctant to confide to friends and associates: "We should have kept quiet."

There was nothing else Dulles could do. The President had spoken and, as a highly responsible member of the Eisenhower Administration, Dulles could not be openly critical of the President.

The blow to Dulles and the CIA was severe. The U-2 spy program, one of the best-kept secrets of our Government's espionage operations, had been bared. The world now knew about one of our most effective tools of espionage, and its precise mechanics.

But beyond the loss of this secret, coupled with the red face our nation had to wear to the shattered Paris Summit meeting, Eisenhower's admission pulled back the curtain of secrecy that had veiled the activities of the CIA. In the days and weeks ahead we learned a great deal more about the super-secret CIA. We were told that this intelligence agency is constantly engaged in espionage the world over as much as the KGB, if not more so.

In time we would learn that CIA agents could be found in such far-off places as remote Tibet, gathering information about Red Chinese troop movements; in Albania, picking up information about the feud between that country's Red leaders and the Kremlin hierarchy; on Taiwan, helping train Chinese Nationalist pilots who some day may fly across the Formosa Straits in the long-expected invasion of Mainland China. Other CIA operatives, disguised in Arab garb, may be taking movie film with telephoto-lensed cameras of atomic blasts being set off by French scientists on the Sahara Desert, and others may be protecting America's interests in Central or South America, doing their part in countering Communist tactics—such as the so-called banana revolt that overthrew the Moscow-oriented government of President Jacobo Arbenz Guzman. And as we learned in 1967, still others may even be financing colleges, publishers, and other American institutions under the guise of patriotism.

The U-2 spy episode and revelations about the CIA's extensive involvement in espionage the world over have done as much to contribute to the Age of Confusion as this country's naiveté had kept it in the Age of Innocence and the Congressional red herring probes had ushered in the Age of Suspicion.

But the Age of Confusion need not continue, if we can understand what we are doing in espionage is a vital function of government to protect our interests and promote the power and welfare of the country. We must spy more now than ever because of the drastic change in the mood and political geography of the world in recent years.

A generation ago our vital interests were not readily subject to attack in every corner of the globe as they seem to be now. Then, we had no idea our military forces would be stationed in South Vietnam, Korea, Japan, West Germany, Turkey, England, Spain, and dozens of other foreign footholds, or that we would have to be alert to hostile elements in Cuba, the Congo, Central and South America, China—even Russia, our World War II ally. We as Americans had lived smugly among ourselves in splendid isolation; we could not predict our vast international involvement that would begin in the late 1930s and proliferate through the 1940s, 1950s, and 1960s.

Today no one can predict where the next danger spot will be, where our reputation and value as a generous world power will suddenly be challenged, when our zealous "progressivism" in the world at large will all at once face a defiant attack requiring our economic and military resources in great strength.

With the danger of missiles and bombers that can be launched by an enemy in minutes, we can no longer rely on proof positive to tell us an enemy is preparing to set off an attack on us. We must be forewarned—even about the danger of losing some remote overseas area such as Cambodia or Thailand. For when the Free World loses one of these areas, it loses a bit more of its security, just as the Communist world is weakened when one of its allies falls into our camp.

We must have our spies the world over to tell us what is going on. But by that same token, the Soviet Union, Red China, Czechoslovakia, and any other foreign power which is not on the same ideological wavelength as the United States and its Free World allies, must do the same. Those nations, too, have every right to look after their own interests—to guard against attack from us, just as we must be prepared to detect a surprise blow from them.

Unfortunately, not all Americans understand this philosophy and many do not condone espionage; they would have us go back to the Age of Suspicion or further, to the Age of Innocence. Many scream and shout that the CIA and the FBI have been allowed to become all too powerful. Many would like Congress to strip these agencies of their authority.

These critics, however, would not be taking us back to the Age of Suspicion or the Age of Innocence. Instead, they would be ushering us into the Age of Stupidity. Perhaps they and their followers are unmindful of the admonition voiced by Allen Dulles in his recent best seller, *The Craft of Intelligence*. Dulles, who wrote the book after his retirement as director of the CIA in 1961, says:

"Clearly, if a country wishes to protect itself against the unceasing encroachments of hostile intelligence services it must do more than keep an eye on foreign travelers crossing its borders, more than placing guards around its 'sensitive' areas, more than checking on the loyalty of its employees in sensitive positions. It must also find out what the intelligence services of hostile countries are after, how they are proceeding and what people they are using. It can best accomplish these tasks by penetrating the inner circle of hostile services where the plans are made and the agents selected and trained, and, if the job can be managed, by bringing over to its side 'insiders' from the other camp."

The present book, coming as it does at a time when the current fictional spy story craze has made espionage a form of romantic escapism instead of the deadly thing that it really is, has attempted to show how the Soviet Union, through its own intelligence operatives, tries and very often succeeds, in bringing over to its side "insiders" from our camp.

It is hoped that these cases of Soviet espionage against the United States will enlighten Americans to the confusion of purpose on the part of that certain small faction in this country who would strip the CIA and the FBI of their functions and areas of responsibility.

Espionage, the author contends, is not a game between the good guys and the bad guys, or between black and white. It is a vital activity conducted by almost every nation against almost every other nation—merely to keep alive in the world community.

We do not wish to go back to the era of naive innocence, nor to the Congressional red-herring days, nor to McCarthyism. This is a simple plea to a country which has passed from the Age of Innocence to the Age of Suspicion to the Age of Confusion, to enter, at last, the Age of Maturity.

Index